On the cover...

...is a child who may represent the future of your life, your family, your business or your career. The man behind him represents the ability to guide your future away from dangers in the background and onto a safer path. The photograph is in black and white because it could have been taken any time in the last fifty years or so. The metaphor is timeless.

Don Osborne

The Probable Future:

You Can Predict it & You Can Change it

Discover the Patterns That Affect
the Future of Your Life, Your Family
and Whole Organizations

Dr. Don Osborne

The Probable Future:

You Can Predict it &
You Can Change it

(Book One in the *Think Then Lead* Series)

Discover the eight interactive patterns that are all around you. There are principles embedded in the patterns that determine how everything happens in your life, in your family, in the groups you belong to, and where you work. You can recognize them to predict and change the probable future!

Dr. Don Osborne

© Copyright 2012 by Donald R. Osborne, Jr.
All rights reserved.
ISBN-10: 1477452036
EAN-13: 9781477452035

This book is dedicated to Krisann Osborne who has pointed out patterns and inspired me to change paths throughout our lives together.

Don Osborne

Acknowledgement

I am deeply indebted to the following people, listed in alphabetical order, who provided editorial advice, coaching, encouragement and reviewed all or parts of this book: Greg Baldauf, Kenneth Ballou, Jeffrey Gitomer, Mark Grisham, Dr. David Magnin, Kelly Medwick, Bob Mason, David Osborne, Krisann Osborne, Stephanie Osborne, Corey Perlman, Angel Rea, Ardy Richards, Dr. Clay Smith, Robin Shanks, and Anna Stevens. They provided perspectives that I could not see and I am grateful.

Don Osborne, EdD

Contents

Introduction
    Can You See the Patterns? 1

Principle One
    Thinking Things Through 11
        Blind Spots. 17
        Key Points & Action You Can Take 21

Principle Two
    Your World View Dictates Your Choices 23
        Remember the Pattern 32
        Three Worldviews Visit a
            Convenience Store 33
        You Can't See Your Own Ears 40
        Key Points & Action You Can Take 43

Principle Three
    You Become What You Think About. 47
        People Who Defeat Themselves
            and People Who Excel 53
        A Case Study 58
        Key Points & Action You Can Take 61

Principle Four
The Only Four Ways That You Interact With Others . . 63
The Need for Approval. 65
The Recipient's Perspective 66
Punishment 69
An Effective Way to Correct Behavior. . . .72
Rewarding by Removing Something
    Unpleasant. 75
Analyzation, Application
    and Effectiveness 77
Key Points & Action You Can Take 80

Principle Five
Systems of Relationships with Predictable Patterns. . .83
Creativity Requires Change
    (and is Therefore Resisted). 86
Change and Change Management. 88
Open and Closed Human Systems 90
Key Points & Action You Can Take 96

Principle Six
The Patterns in Developmental Stages 99
Human Development. 101
Stages of Commitment. 104
Developmental Stages of Groups
    and Teams 108
Stages of Separation, Grief and Loss 112
Stages of Organizational Development. .117
Stages of Moral Development 122
Key Points & Action You Can Take 128

Principle Seven
    Whom Do You Serve?..........................131
        Stakeholders and Sustainability.........133
        Absolutes and Doing the Right Thing...139
        Key Points & Action You Can Take....142

Principle Eight
    Living an Intentional Life Has Risks..............145
        Consider the Following Examples......151
        Vision, Risk, Plans and Perseverance...155
        Key Points & Action You Can Take....160

Epilogue
    Develop the Wisdom to Predict
    and Change Your Future.....................163

Introduction

Can You See the Patterns?

"*He's always working! He's never home; I never see him. The kids hardly know him. He's a workaholic.*"

"*I'm just trying to provide for my family. I want them to have the things I never had when growing up. She doesn't appreciate the sacrifices I'm making so she can be a stay-at-home mom, which we both want. But somebody has to work so that she can do that. We've got a nice house, two cars, a boat, a place at the lake, and our kids will be able to go to college.*"

I had heard it all a hundred times before. It was all so predictable I even knew what the next words were going to be.

"The kids and I would rather have you than all the material things."

The Probable Future

This marriage was in trouble and the future was probably going to be the same as dozens of others I had seen unless something very different happened. Reason has nothing to do in situations like this. People are acting on emotion and using logic to justify their choices and behavior. It was time to try something to veer this pattern off of its destructive path...

If you roll a ball on a level floor, it will follow a straight path. Before it reaches the other side of the room, you can see where it is headed. If you don't want the ball to continue in that direction, you can tap it and send it veering off in a different direction. Your life is like that.

...So, I turned to Rick, the workaholic, and asked what hours he usually worked. Predictably, Helen, his wife, answered for him and said he left the house at 7:00 AM each day and didn't get home until about 7:30 PM each evening. I asked Helen to let Rick answer the questions I asked him. Then I asked Rick why he felt the need to spend such long hours at work. He replied that there was so much to do, that he couldn't get it all done. In fact, each day when he came home, he still left much that needed to be done at work. I suggested that Rick go in to work an hour earlier each day. Helen jumped up and nearly screwed her head into the ceiling. I calmed her down and asked her to just go along and give Rick a chance. He thought for a moment, and said,"Yeah, that would be six more hours a week and I could probably catch up." The couple left

with the understanding that Rick would work an extra hour each day by getting up and off to work an hour earlier. Helen wasn't happy, but agreed not to nag him for the next week until they saw me again.

The next week, predictably, nothing had changed. Rick was going in an hour earlier but was still behind at work at the end of each day. So, I said to Rick, "Why not go in another hour earlier. Maybe you can catch up then." Helen's jaw dropped. Rick stared at me, wondering if I was serious. Then, slowly, he considered it. Finally, he said, "OK, it's worth a shot." He would leave the house by 5:00 AM to go to work every day for the next week and be home by 7:30 PM.

The next week, Helen was strangely quiet. Rick was obviously exhausted. He reported that he was going in at 5:00 AM before anyone else got to work, putting in fourteen hours and coming home worn out. Still, he was leaving work with some tasks not completed and he was making more mistakes. I suggested going in at 4:00 AM. Rick looked at me hard without saying anything for several seconds. Then he said, "That's crazy." I agreed with him and asked him to decide where the craziness begins and ends. Rick finally realized that no matter how many hours he put in at work, there would always be something that still needed to be done. He broke the pattern and changed his lifestyle. The last I saw Rick and Helen, they were with their children picking up things at the store for a weekend camping trip. They were laughing. Rick only works about 45 hours a week now. He veered off of a destructive path and changed the probable future for himself and his family.

If you could see what is probably going to happen in your personal future, in the futures of your children, or in the future of your organization, would you want to know it? It's not very hard to predict what's going to happen.

It is amazing how accurately you can predict what is going to happen when you see patterns. It is also amazing that more people don't recognize them as they are happening. Perhaps they don't always stand back and look at the big picture. Repeated patterns become predictable paths into the future. If the patterns don't change, then they become the future.

First, you have to recognize the path that you are on. Your employer's path, the path that your marriage is on, and the paths that your career and personal life are on result from repeated patterns of thinking and behaving. Have you ever had someone say, "I know what you're going to do" and you got angry because she was right? Other people might see your patterns of thinking and behaving more easily than you can see your own. And you can usually see other people's patterns better than they can see them in themselves.

Have you ever watched kids argue?
"You're doing that wrong."
"I am not. I'm doing it my way."
"You're stupid."
"Shut up."
"Don't tell me to shut up. You shut up."

Can You See the Patterns?

Could you predict where the conversation was going after the second remark was made? You know that when one says something in a certain familiar tone of voice that the other youngster is going to retaliate with a similar remark. Then the predictable pattern of arguing that they have developed over dozens of similar occasions is underway. Communication patterns are so predictable that libraries are full of books on the subject. Communication between you and your friends and between you and people where you work follows patterns. In fact, there are patterns all around you.

Professional football quarterbacks are paid a great deal of money for their ability to "read defenses" and see the patterns in the opposing teams. They recognize the opposing teams' defensive formation patterns...where different defensive players are on the field. Some quarterbacks are more athletic than others are, and some are more accurate at passing the football. The ones usually judged the best, however, are the quarterbacks that can accurately predict what the opposing team is going to do defensively. They then counter that with an unexpected offensive play. Professional quarterbacks develop that skill by studying their game and seeing the patterns of defensive formations hundreds of times.

Investors that make fortunes with their financial predictions recognize patterns in how corporations perform, or how the stock market performs over time. The really good ones study the things that have happened repeatedly and can fairly accurately figure out the right time to buy stock in a particular company. Warren Buffet, regarded by many as the most successful investor ever was described in his biography, *The Snowball*, as spending a great deal of time studying the patterns of corporations' performance over time. He studied the management style that was in place, market conditions, etc. until he could very accurately predict what would happen if he were to invest in them. As a result, he amassed an immense fortune and was, at one time, the wealthiest man in the world.

Trained and experienced counselors can pretty accurately predict what is going to happen in a client's life if changes aren't made. After working with a couple of hundred clients and their families, patterns become very familiar. In fact, many books have also been written about some of those recognizable behavior patterns. With just a little training, you can see the patterns in your own life as well as predict what family, friends, co-workers and the company you work for are probably going to do in time.

Bill, the guy next door to me in the freshman dorm, came over to my room excitedly insisting that I had to double date with him. In an effort to control traffic congestion, the university did not allow us freshmen to have cars on campus. Bill's date was also a freshman without a car, but her roommate was a sophomore who had her own vehicle. Bill was majoring in music and knew his girlfriend's roommate because she was also a music major. He convinced me to walk the two miles to where the girls lived on Friday night. As we walked into the parking lot, a young woman came down the outside stairs from the second floor with a mop and a bucket in hand. She had short dark hair, wore cat-eye glasses which were popular at the time, and she wore jeans rolled up to her shins. Apparently, she had just mopped up an overflowing toilet in the room above hers. "This is your date, Don," and with that, Bill disappeared through the front door of the girls' dorm. Her name was Krisann and she knew nothing about a double date. She said, "I'm not going on any date tonight." I stood there all dressed up in the most stylish clothes that I had, sweaty from the two-mile walk. I looked her in the eye and said, "I had a hunch you wouldn't go out with me when I got here." She stared back for a moment and said, "You wait right here." Much faster than I ever remembered a girl getting ready for anything, Krisann came back out the front door looking gorgeous. She was tall and slender with the longest legs I had ever seen. Using her car, we double dated that night with Bill and Krisann's roommate.

We were both broke college students and, as a music major, Krisann practiced for her quarterly piano recital every evening. Our "dates" settled into a routine…a pattern. We would meet in the cafeteria on campus for an evening meal and then we were off to the music building. Practice rooms were only big enough to hold a studio piano and one plastic chair. Her recital piece that semester was Debussy's Arabesque No. 1. I sat on the floor of the practice room pretending to read my assignments while she practiced and played that lilting piece over and over. Looking over the edge of a book, I stared at the intensity on her face and fell in love for the very first time. For the first couple of months that we knew each other, that was our pattern.

After a stormy two and a half year relationship, we both ran out of money to go to college, so we got married. The first few years were rough. I had a drinking problem and we were always short money. We moved around to avoid problems that my drinking created. We sold the piano that Krisann's parents had bought for her when she was in Jr. High School. A few years later I stopped drinking just three days before Krisann delivered our son. I broke my pattern, changed paths and went back to school to finish my undergraduate degree. Sober, I was finally able to hold a job more than a few months and our lives improved. I earned a Master's degree and became a counselor. We got an old upright piano from a church that had bought a new piano. Krisann wanted so badly to play again. Not long thereafter, our daughter was born. Our lives settled down and we raised our family. Ball games, dance recitals, and my career kept us busy. Krisann went back to school, finished her college degree and later earned a Master's degree, as well. I earned a second Master's degree and a doctorate along the way. Becoming a little more affluent, I surprised Krisann on her birthday with a grand piano.

The children are grown and have families of their own. It's just the two of us now and we have settled into a familiar routine. Some patterns have not changed. Krisann plays the piano whenever she can; it is her passion. Every now and again, her fingers

Can You See the Patterns?

remember the notes to Debussy's Arabesque No. 1. Wherever I am in the house when she plays that lilting melody, I gravitate toward the piano room. I'll sit down and stare at the intensity on Krisann's face as she plays from memory. And fall in love for the very first time. Again.

This book describes eight interactive patterns that overlap with each other and determine how you function as an individual, in your family, in groups to which you belong, and in your work. By recognizing and understanding the patterns, it becomes possible for you to predict the probable future. You can then make choices and decisions based on what will probably happen, and what will likely happen after that. If you apply the *principles* embedded in the patterns, you can not only change your own path, but also influence those around you. You can alter the probable future from what it is going to be to what you want it to be.

It's like tapping a ball rolling on the floor and changing its direction.

Principle One

Thinking Things Through

While working as a counselor with troubled kids in Michigan, I was approached by a boy about fourteen years old who defiantly announced that he was going to run away. He came to me and volunteered that information. He said that he had not told anyone else, and his announcement to me seemed like a challenge. "Let's see you talk me out of this one," he seemed to be saying. I knew from years of experience and training that if I tried to talk him out of his decision, he would just become more resolved to run away. Instead I simply asked him to tell me about his decision. He was in a foster home, the most recent of a long list of placements by the state because his parents were incarcerated for drug dealing. The boy, I'll call him John,

The Probable Future

acknowledged that the couple he was living with were nice people and were kind and even affectionate toward him, but they wouldn't let him run the streets, smoke or do as he pleased.

John was used to an unstructured, undisciplined life and chafed against even reasonable rules. So, he said, he had a cousin about his same age that lived in Texas and John had investigated the cost of a bus ticket from Michigan to the town in Texas. He seemed quite proud that he had thought out such a bold plan. He had acquired the bus ticket money somehow. After school, instead of going home, he was going to go to the bus station, buy a ticket and ride the bus to the town in Texas where his cousin lived. I congratulated John on thinking things through and he smiled smugly.

I then asked him, "What will happen then, John?"

He looked a bit stunned, thought for a moment and said, "I'll call my aunt and uncle and they'll come and get me at the bus station."

"Okay, John" I said, "What will happen then?"

Puzzling for a while, he then replied, "They'll take me home but they'll probably be really ticked off, 'cause they won't know I'm coming."

"So what do you think will happen next, John?" I asked.

"They'll call the authorities back up here," he said.

"So, then what?"

"The Michigan juvenile authorities will come and get me and bring me back up here."

"What do you think will happen after that, John?"

"They'll put me back in the same foster home I'm in now."

"Then what?"

"They'll all be really ticked off at me."

Then John said, "This isn't going to work, is it?"

I said, "John, I think you're right."

For perhaps the first time in his life, the 14 year old boy with the deck stacked against him thought something all the way through. He arrived at his own conclusion, and rightly decided that running away was not a good idea. Two lessons are important here. I didn't tell John that he was being stupid or that his plan was faulty and therefore didn't give him more to rebel against. He thought it through without criticism from an adult authority figure, so it was his own ultimate decision. Secondly, without being judged, he simply was encouraged to think of what would likely happen next, and then what would happen after that. Fervently do I wish that I had someone asking me that simple question, "What will likely happen next?" at many points in my own life.

Have you ever played chess? The winner is usually the player that can plot the most moves in advance. The great Russian grand master and former world chess champion Garry Kasparov was once asked how many moves he calculated in advance. He replied that three to five moves ahead was pretty normal but, depending on the situation on the chess board, he could think up to twelve or fourteen moves ahead. Remember that each move was dependent on

The Probable Future

the moves that his opponent might make. Therefore, he could think of twelve or more moves that he would make based on the numerous choices of moves that his opponent would likely make. If his opponent considered three different moves each time he had a turn, then Mr. Kasparov was planning his next move based on each of his opponent's choices. He was, therefore, actually thinking about the possibility of perhaps fifty moves. You have the ability to think ahead, too. Do you usually think ahead far enough?

Dan Renn was a brilliant young entrepreneur in the Southeast in the late 1960's and early 1970's. By the age of 30, he was a multi-millionaire. Dan had bought the rights to market and sell a simple fire alarm. It contained a plug in a tube that melted at 136° Fahrenheit and allowed liquid Freon in a connected canister to turn into Freon gas, flow through the tube and through a horn, making an effective and loud alarm. Selling them door-to-door, Dan recruited a sales force that took off, well, like a fire. Renn Enterprises, Ltd. had a direct sales force numbering hundreds in a dozen states when Dan backed a home safety group that lobbied for fire alarms to be placed in all newly constructed homes and buildings. The legislation passed, and within a few months, all of the large national retailers were carrying ionization or smoke detectors for half the price of what Renn Enterprises could sell their antiquated alarms. Building contractors bought detectors directly from manufacturers with the latest technology. Owners of homes built before the legislation passed could buy two detectors with the latest technology for what one of Dan's fire alarms cost. Within a short time, Renn Enterprises, Ltd. was out of business.

Dan Renn was a master salesman, but he didn't think far enough ahead. He helped lobby for legislation that put him out of business. Dan probably didn't think about the enormous competition and innovative technology that a legislated market would create. Rather than pursuing business success again, Dan Renn devoted the remainder of his life to helping others through the Peace Corps and through his church.

Jim Holdren was a very successful businessman in Indiana who provided some much needed mentoring on finance and running a business when I was a young man. I asked Jim his formula for making the right decisions and he said, "I always play the odds." When I asked him to explain, Jim said that he looked at what had happened in the past in his own experience and also what he knew had happened to other businesses or people in the same situation he was confronted with before he decided anything. For example, he said, all of the safety statistics on hundreds of thousands of drivers and passengers point to the fact that people are much more likely to survive automobile accidents if they wear safety belts, so he always wore a safety belt when in a car. He didn't wear a safety belt because it was legally mandated. He wore one because the odds were in his favor if he did. His worldview was both positive and realistic. He could learn from the mistakes of others.

The Probable Future

Jim always looked at what would probably happen if he chose one course of action over another. He owned grocery stores and knew his business very well. He knew when a competing grocery store moved into town what would likely happen. Jim plotted his pricing strategies accordingly. He and his staff designed an innovative marketing approach to counter the new competitor's arrival in town. Because he knew his business so well and thought so far ahead, his own business continued to thrive despite the new competition. Jim knew and understood the life cycles that businesses go through. He knew the stage of development his own company was in, and knew that his new competitor would be in a start-up stage and the challenges that they faced. Jim's employees and customers remained loyal to him because he knew them and treated them well. Jim's ability to predict what would probably happen kept him in business making a sound profit until much later when he sold his stores and retired.

> "Make sure you are right, then go ahead."
>
> — *Davy Crockett*
>
> American Frontiersman and US Congressman, killed at the battle of the Alamo

Bob and Gary were two addicts who radically changed their lives. They used to drink and use various street drugs together, and both had arrest records. One weekend, they decided to drive to a city not too far away to attend a rock concert. Jokingly, Bob said, "Should we pick up a case of beer to drink on the trip?" Gary replied, "Sure, and I know where we can get some weed (marijuana) too." Then Bob said, "Oh, while we're at it, let's pick up some crack (cocaine). I know where we can get it." Gary then said, "Okay, let's go ahead and call our lawyers in advance, and arrange our bail before we get underway," and they both laughed. The two recovering addicts were talking about a very familiar pattern in their lives. They knew that drinking and using drugs would result in their doing something that would attract the attention of the police, and they would be arrested again. They had learned to recognize their own patterns, and they chose to change the patterns and their probable futures.

Blind Spots

Although people have the capacity to reason, many don't seem to think things through, and so, make bad decisions and create problems for themselves and the people around them. Good judgment is said to come from experience that was largely made up of bad judgment. Maturity may be defined, then, as the use of good judgment so that you don't make the same mistakes again.

The Probable Future

A farmer walking through his cornfield came upon a rattlesnake. Snakes eat mice and other vermin in cornfields so the farmer decided to leave the rattlesnake alone but then it spoke to him. The snake said to the farmer, "Please pick me up and put me in your pocket and walk across the road. If I try to cross the road on my own, I may be run over by a car. If you put me down in your cornfield on the other side of the road, I'll eat the mice over there so that they don't destroy your crop." The farmer was astonished at first that the rattlesnake spoke to him, but believed what he said, and so he picked the snake up and put him in his pocket. Once across the road, the farmer reached into his pocket to get the snake, and the snake bit him as the farmer lowered him to the ground. The farmer screamed in pain and then yelled at the snake, "Why did you bite me? I did you a favor and carried you across the road in my pocket and you repaid me by biting me!" The snake replied, "You knew I was a rattlesnake when you picked me up."

Wisdom is learning from your own history as well as learning from the histories of others so that you also avoid making the mistakes that other people have made. Wisdom comes from recognizing patterns in the way that you and everyone else functions as individuals, in families, in groups, and in organizations. You gain a perspective of what is probably going to happen before it actually happens.

You may be blind to the patterns around you more often than you see them. People close to you may try to point out a predictable pattern and a probable future course of events that you cannot or will not see for yourself.

Friends and relatives watched in great distress as Anna began visiting an incarcerated felon. She met him when her church mission group went to the state prison and handed out Bibles to inmates. Ronnie was a repeat offender that had been married and divorced four times, and had often been jailed for domestic battery on his wives. He was currently in prison for assault with a deadly weapon. Ronnie was 44 and Anna was 19 years old. Anna believed Ronnie when he told her that he felt closer to God because of her visits. So, she continued to visit him without her church group and began writing to him while he was in prison. At his request, Anna began leaving money at the office so that Ronnie could buy snacks from the prison commissary, which he then traded for favors with other inmates. The other church group members, her pastor, her parents and friends all tried to warn Anna that Ronnie was a dangerous man with a history of preying on young women. Anna told everyone that she was in love with him and that Ronnie told her that he was in love with her and would change. "He said that he would change for me if I will just trust him." A few months later, the two were married while Ronnie was still incarcerated. Anna waited two more years for him to be released. Six months later, Ronnie beat her so severely that she was in the hospital for several weeks and nearly died. She refused to press charges, *and when she got out of the hospital, she went back to him.*

Why couldn't Anna see what was probably going to happen? Why didn't she leave Ronnie after he beat her so severely? It has to do with the way that Anna sees the world and interprets things that go on around her. The next chapter explains why we are sometimes blind to patterns and the principles they hold.

Thinking Things Through

Key Points & Action You Can Take

You're capable of thinking ahead and using logic and your experience from the past to figure out what will likely happen in any situation. Although you have the ability to think ahead, you may not use it to your greatest advantage. You may be blind to some patterns in your life that other people can see in you.

1. Research what has happened to others that were faced with circumstances similar to yours. You might learn from their mistakes and successes.
2. Whenever possible, seek the experience and training of experts in the area before making big decisions.
3. Learn as much as possible about patterns of behavior that have been observed and documented. Study interpersonal patterns of behavior as well as the way that groups of people and organizations operate. You will find a lot of that information in this book.
4. Become introspective and think back on how you have handled relationships and situations in your past. Decide whether you are repeating mistakes that cause difficulties for you and others.
5. Decide what you might need to change in the way that you approach people and problem solving.

6. Study the patterns of thinking and behaving outlined in this book. Think of ways to apply them to your own life.
7. After gathering as much input as you can through research, you can ask yourself, "What will likely happen next?", and then, "What will happen after that?" If you do that for twelve to fourteen choices ahead, you might achieve the chess master Garry Kasparov's success in your own endeavors.

Principle Two

Your Worldview Dictates Your Choices

As a young man, I experienced overwhelming difficulties in my life and decided to move away somewhere and start over. I had lost several jobs, I drank too much, my marriage was shaky and we were deeply in debt. I was convinced that I had started my adult life in the wrong part of the country and had the wrong kind of friends. So, my wife and I moved a thousand miles away "to be nearer to her family." In some circles, this is called "taking a geographic cure." It's the idea that problems you experience in life are related to where you live. If you move somewhere else, you shouldn't have those problems. Well, *within six months after moving, I had already lost a job, had become friends with people just like me, and had exactly the same problems that I had where we lived before. Unfortunately, when we moved I took myself along to the new location. The problems were not caused by the place in the world where I lived...they were caused by how I viewed the world and responded to it.*

How did you develop your view of yourself and the world around you? Why do some people have such a negative view or one that creates problems for themselves and the people close to them? Why do some folks have a positive view and seem to enjoy life and flourish wherever they are? Perhaps the answer is best understood by examining the *worldview* from which you operate. Germans call it *Weltanschauung*. It means your perspective of how the world works.

Think of your mind as being divided between your conscious awareness, and your subconscious. Your subconscious contains your beliefs about how the world works, your attitudes and biases, and your deepest image of yourself. Those things, collectively referred to here as your "worldview", became the filter through which you now perceive and interpret the world around you.

Conscious
Subconscious

Your Worldview Dictates Your Choices

You are not always aware of what lurks in your subconscious. Your worldview was shaped from birth by both spoken and unspoken messages. For example, if you were born into a family with a mother and a father that both wanted and loved you, your parents probably held and cuddled you. They tended to your needs, spent time with you, cooed at you, etc. Think of the experience and very different set of messages that you received if you were unwanted...if you were born into a situation where your parents were negligent, absent or abusive. Growing up, the family played a vital role in letting you know if you were loved, wanted and considered to be of value. Later on, the larger environment added more spoken and unspoken messages that determined how you see yourself and your place in the world. Your experiences with other kids at school and the skills you developed or failed to develop had an influence. Maybe you were athletic or had difficulty reading. How people around you reacted to those skills contributed to your development of a belief system about who you are and how the world works. Think of what you were exposed to on TV and in movies. What you heard expressed as opinions and beliefs at home, at school or in religious settings all contributed to the messages that make up your view of the world. Your beliefs about whether or not there is a God, the differences between political parties, the roles of men and women, which auto manufacturer is best, what makes people attractive, and the meaning of life are all shaped by the messages you have been exposed to in your lifetime.

The Probable Future

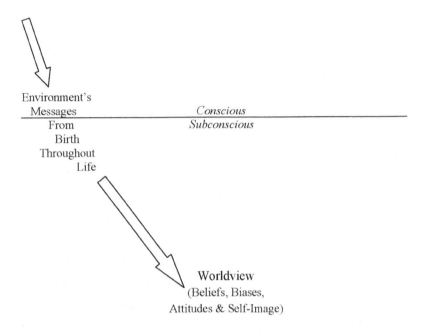

Your worldview dictates the values you developed. Values are based on belief systems, whether formally taught or absorbed through cultural messages. Those people that choose to believe in a benevolent supreme being usually have value systems based on their spiritual beliefs. Atheists and agnostics are left to develop value systems based on their beliefs about the worth of humankind and the meaning of life that they get from their families and the popular culture.

Your Worldview Dictates Your Choices

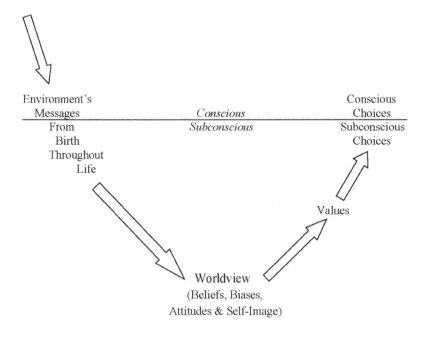

Your values became the parameters or boundaries for the choices you make. You are aware of some choices that you make, but other choices are made without much conscious thought. Instead, the choice comes from thoughts in your subconscious. Some choices are pondered over and some are made on the spur of the moment. Whether consciously thought about or arrived at spontaneously, choices always reflect values. Sometimes, however, choices are weighed out on the basis of two or more conflicting values. The stronger value will always win.

The Probable Future

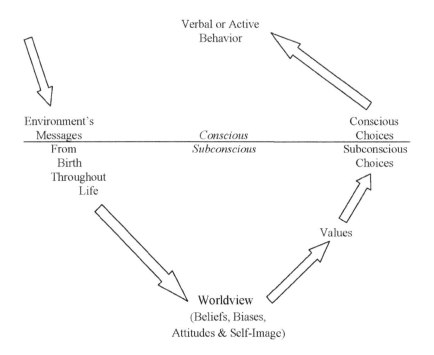

Choices result in behavior, both verbal and active. Every time that you do anything or say anything, it reflects either a conscious or subconscious choice that you have made. All behaviors have outcomes or consequences. Generally, the better the behavior, as perceived by the people around you, the better the outcome. Conversely, the worse the behavior, as perceived by the people around you, the worse the consequences.

Your Worldview Dictates Your Choices

You always interpret the outcomes or consequences you experience according to your worldview.

Your interpretation of the outcomes or consequences of your behavior become a part of the messages feeding into your worldview. Therefore, your worldview provides justification and rationalization for your behavior. You will not change your behavior because of the consequences you experience. You will only change your behavior if your worldview changes.

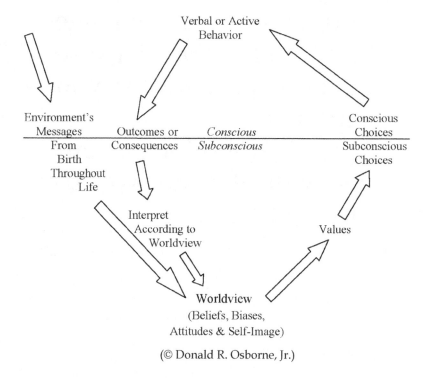

(© Donald R. Osborne, Jr.)

If every day you tell a very smart child that she is stupid, that message will eventually become a part of how she sees herself. It will become a part of her self-image in her worldview. She will make choices in her life and behave in ways that align with how she sees herself. If she believes that she is stupid, she will make illogical choices and act stupidly. She will experience the consequences of acting stupid. She will interpret her consequences from the viewpoint of a girl that thinks of herself as being stupid. Her whole life will be self-defeating unless something changes in the way that she sees herself.

> You will not change your behavior because of the consequences you experience.
> You will only change your behavior if your worldview changes.
>
> — *Don Osborne*

Worldview is difficult to change because it determines how you interpret what you see, hear and

Your Worldview Dictates Your Choices

experience. You do things that align with or are congruent with your worldview even if it creates pain and difficulties for you. For example, people that get out of abusive relationships will often subconsciously seek another abuser. That life is familiar and fits with how they think the world works. It is predictable and therefore oddly comfortable and preferable to the unknown. People that smoke cigarettes, drink alcohol heavily or use other drugs generally see themselves in their self-images as people that do those things. In other words, smokers that try to quit smoking see themselves as smokers who just aren't smoking right now. Smoking is normal for them and to not smoke is contrary to their view of who they are. Their image of themselves is very much a part of their worldview. In order for smokers to successfully quit smoking and remain abstinent, they must come to see themselves as non-smokers for whom smoking would be out of character and not a part of who they are. That means that their deepest image of themselves embedded in their worldview must change in order for them to permanently quit smoking. One of the reasons that Alcoholics Anonymous works so well is that attending daily AA meetings provides a steady stream of new messages. They get absorbed into the subconscious and reshape the drinker's worldview. In time, alcoholics that attend AA often begin to see themselves as people that no longer drink alcohol instead of people that normally drink but just aren't doing so right now. Unless that self-image change occurs in the worldview, the drinker will probably return to drinking.

Remember the Pattern

- You are programmed from birth with messages that are given to you both directly and indirectly through your environment and the people in your life.
- When you receive the same message consistently, it seeps into your subconscious mind and there it shapes your beliefs about how the world works, your attitudes, your biases, and your self-image. Together, they become your worldview, the filter through which you think and interpret reality.
- Your worldview becomes the basis for your values, and your values shape the choices you make.
- Your choices dictate your behavior, the things that you do and say, and generally conform to your values. Sometimes, however, you may be in a position where you have two conflicting values. Whatever action you choose will conflict with one of them.
- Your behavior always has outcomes or consequences. Generally speaking, when you choose "good" behavior, you experience "good" outcomes, and when you choose "bad" behavior, you get "bad" consequences.
- One of the most misunderstood realities, however, is that you will not change your behavior just because of the outcomes and consequences. *That is because you interpret the outcomes and consequences of your behavior according to your worldview.*

Three Worldviews Visit a Convenience Store

Let's look at a man named Jim who grew up believing that life is a pretty negative experience. If you asked him, he would say something like, "Life sucks, and then you die." His belief is that society's institutions are rigged to favor the rich and powerful. Jim believes that there is no such thing as "right" or "wrong", only what one can get away with. He considers the police and judges as hypocritical crooks who use their positions in society to escape accountability. He thinks that they get away with doing the same things that he would get arrested and locked up for doing. Jim does not believe that hard work produces positive rewards. He feels that people with wealth and position use their influence and power to keep people like him from joining their ranks, regardless of how hard a person works. This man does not trust anyone. His value is to survive any way he can. He justifies his choices and behavior with the attitude that he is simply doing what he has to do to get by. "I'm just doing what I've got to do." Jim believes that all men in the same circumstances will choose to act in exactly the same way that he does. He blames his circumstances on other people and events he cannot control. When asked about spiritual beliefs, Jim says, "If there is a God, He hasn't done anything for me." Let's say that this man, Jim, walks into a convenience store late at night, and no one is in sight. The only store employee is in the back room putting up stock, and the cash register till has been left open with money in plain sight. Jim grabs the money, stuffs it into his pocket and walks out of the store. The clerk walks back into the store from the stock room, notices that the till is open and empty, and calls the police. The videotape from the surveillance cameras clearly shows Jim stealing the money. Several blocks down the street, police stop Jim, arrest him, and take him to jail. While being booked into the jail for robbery, Jim is indignant and belligerent, swearing that he has been set up. "It's entrapment," he says. "If they didn't want the money taken, why did they leave it out there? You cops are in on it. You set me up just so you could put me in your jail and hold me down." Jim's worldview is the filter through which he interprets the consequences of his chosen behavior. Indeed, his worldview shapes how he sees what has happened. It reinforces itself with an interpretation that is consistent with Jim's beliefs about how the world works. When he gets out of jail, Jim is likely to commit other crimes because his thinking has not changed.

Now let's look at Bob, a religious man raised to believe that there is a God that set absolute standards about what is right and what is wrong. Bob believes that there are good and bad people, determined largely by each individual's relationship with God. He is convinced that, put in the same circumstances, people will act differently depending on their beliefs about what is right and wrong. Bob believes that it

Your Worldview Dictates Your Choices

is always wrong to steal. He recognizes that he lives in an imperfect world with imperfect people, but it is his choice to give people the benefit of the doubt. He sees life as an adventure, a journey filled with opportunities either to adhere to his beliefs and values or to ignore them. Although he knows that some police officers and some judges act unethically, he believes that they are in the minority. It is his responsibility as a good citizen to cooperate with society's institutions. Bob believes that hard work yields positive results, sooner or later. He does not believe it proper to expect something for nothing. For that reason, Bob does not even buy lottery tickets. "If I won it, I wouldn't feel right because I didn't earn it," he would say. Now, this man walks into the same convenience store late at night. Again, the only store clerk is in the back room putting up stock. The cash register till has been left open with money in plain sight. Bob calls out, "Hey is anybody here? You left the till open." When the clerk hurries back into the store from the stock room, Bob laughingly says, "I could have walked out of here with all that money. You need to be more careful." Bob's worldview dictated his values. It set the parameters or boundaries for the choice he made. He alerted the store clerk that the cash register till was open. As a result, the clerk was very grateful and praised Bob for his honesty and for saving the clerk's job. After making his purchase Bob walks out of the convenience store feeling pretty good about himself. That experience further reinforces the personal convictions that determined his behavior.

In a third scenario, let's say that a man named John believes the same way that Bob believes. In fact, they attend the same church together. However, John was laid off from his job over a year ago, and he has not been able to find steady work ever since. His wife had a baby during the last year, and they were without health insurance. John's three older children are all in school and he was unable to afford them new shoes when they started the new school year. His savings are long gone, and he is filled with despair. John's pride prevents him from seeking help from his church or social agencies. He goes to the same convenience store to buy a quart of milk for the baby with some change he has found. The same clerk is in the back room putting up stock. The till has been left open with money in plain sight. Now remember, John believes that it is wrong to steal. He is a religious man and believes in a standard of absolute right and wrong. However, because of his circumstances, he has conflicting values... it is wrong to steal, but he is responsible for providing for his family. Any choice that he makes will conflict with one of his values. John makes an exception to his moral code and steals the money, puts it in his pocket and walks out of the store. The clerk returns, sees that the till is open and the money is gone, and calls the police. The videotape from the surveillance cameras shows John stealing the money. The police soon arrest John and take him to jail. While being booked into the jail, John laments, "I knew I shouldn't have done it. I knew it was wrong." John feels that he is getting what he deserves for stealing, despite his family's desperate financial circumstances. Humbled, he believes that he should have found some other way to provide for his family by seeking assistance. He could have sought help from his church or a social agency. John is convinced that he made the wrong decision because now he has legal trouble in addition to his financial woes. He may be incarcerated and even less able to help his family. His behavior was an exception to his normal pattern, since his core thinking did not change. John interprets his consequences according to his worldview. He expresses remorse for behaving in a way that conflicted with his values, and is unlikely ever to break the law again.

In all three scenarios, Jim, Bob and John interpreted the consequences of their behavior according to their worldviews. Their thinking made perfect sense, given their belief systems. Even though they arrived at different conclusions, their logic was not faulty. The difference was in their beliefs, attitudes, biases, and self-images.

Several years ago public school systems in the USA began realizing that students' behavior was becoming increasingly dangerous. At the same time, however, the authority of schools to administer consequences for unacceptable behavior was reduced. Across the country, schools began buying packaged programs designed to help kids make good choices. Those programs, however, did not change the trend of students threatening other students and teachers. Bullying, inappropriate sexual behavior, and being dangerous has actually increased. Schools were reluctant to teach values because values stem from worldview, which includes belief systems. Finally, schools decided to teach values, but not connect them with any belief system. There are posters in schools today that encourage students to "Treat each other with kindness." But they have no connection to a foundational system of beliefs. There is nothing that says why they should be kind or even how to define "kindness". The results can be read in newspapers and seen on TV news shows. Public schools continue to be places where bullying, threats of violence and inappropriate sexual behavior is common.

Your worldview ultimately determines your behavior. It then reinforces itself by being the filter through which you interpret the consequences of your behavior.

- If you wish to change your consequences, you must change your behavior.
- In order to change your behavior, you must change the pattern of choices that you make.
- To change your choices, you must change your values.
- To change your values, you must change your worldview.

Your Worldview Dictates Your Choices

The good news is that it is quite possible for you to change your worldview. It is not easy, but it is possible. By doing so, you can dramatically alter the path your life is on. It begins with the recognition that you are experiencing a *pattern* of consequences, and then accepting that only you are responsible for the behavior that leads to those consequences. Secondly, you must see that your behavior is determined by your thinking. Your thinking is the result of influences since birth, but you have the ability to change the way that you think. You can reprogram your thinking by choosing to expose yourself to different messages that will alter your worldview. Unfortunately, people tend not to try this unless they reach a point of desperation as a result of the consequences they face.

> You are responsible for your own thinking, choices and behavior, and I am responsible for mine.
>
> — *Don Osborne*

You Can't See Your Own Ears

One of the problems you face with your worldview, values, choices and behavior is that you cannot observe yourself objectively. You cannot get outside of yourself to see what your attitude and behavior look like. You cannot rely on your perception of yourself to be accurate. Just as you cannot see your own ears, you cannot see your own attitudes and behavior the way that other people see you. You need other people to reflect back to you how you come across to them.

There was a young man who didn't realize that he was generally regarded as obnoxious by those with whom he came in contact. He genuinely thought other people were jealous of him because he saw himself as superior to others. He believed that he was irresistible to women, and that his views on just about everything were brilliant. Other people saw him as conceited, self-centered, arrogant and condescending. After an encounter with this young man, most people avoided him. He interpreted that it was because everyone was envious of his superiority. He thought they were in awe of him. Because of a series of enormous problems occurring in his life due to his personality disorder, he agreed to counseling. He was truly baffled by the way that other people regarded him in a therapy group, however. Only after numerous group therapy sessions was he aware of his problem. It has sometimes been called the "green tail" analogy. If someone tells you that you have a green tail, you may well imagine that he has been smoking something illegal. If a second person tells you that you have a green tail, then you might believe that she is smoking the same thing with the other guy. However, if several people from different walks of life tell you that you have a green tail, then you had best turn around to see what is dragging on the ground behind you.

The first genuine compliment that the young man in the therapy group received was, "Gee, you're not nearly as big a jerk as you were a couple of months ago." Originally, this young man could not see himself as he came across to others. It required an unusual situation in which new messages about who he was and how other people saw him finally penetrated his well-defended self-image deep in his subconscious. With other people reflecting back to him how he came across, once he understood it and believed it, he was open to change. Over time, his worldview did change, and he eventually became a person that other people found interesting. He became genuinely interested in other people. His whole life turned around. His marriage flourished and his ability to engage other people appropriately and interact in proper relationships developed as it should have when he was growing up.

In order for you to see yourself as others see you and not just the way that you want to see yourself, you must give people permission and invite them to confront you with how they see you. You must be careful, though, who you invite to be honest with you.

- Don't choose people that will always agree with you or try to flatter you, like acquaintances that don't know you well or people who are afraid of offending you.
- Don't choose people that will use your permission and invitation to be honest with you as a means to emotionally abuse you. Avoid people with whom you have had strong disagreements, or who don't want you to confront them in return.

> It is incredibly important to realize through this principle that your perception of yourself is rarely accurate unless it has been tested against how other people see you. Choose your accountability partners well.
>
> — *Don Osborne*

Key Points & Action You Can Take

The programming you received from birth through spoken and unspoken messages has shaped your worldview. It is the filter through which you perceive and interpret reality. You did not get to choose your initial programming that ultimately shaped your personality, but you can alter it. In order to benefit from this principle, you must come to know yourself well. The following suggestions may help.

1. As you realize more about how your worldview has been shaped, you may see how your choices and behavior have been predictable to others that have known you.
2. Decide the kind of person you want to become and the kind of life that you want to have. Accept responsibility for altering your worldview to the greatest benefit for yourself and those close to you.
3. Review your attitudes, beliefs and biases. Try to figure out where they came from. Keep the ones that you want to keep and discard the rest by telling yourself repeatedly that they have no further relevance to the person you have chosen to become.
4. Avoid influences that are toxic to you. If you know people that are very critical of you, or who are negative about most things in general, stay away from them. Don't listen to music,

read books or watch TV shows or movies that influence you to feel or think negatively.
5. Intentionally choose the kind of influences that you want to seep into your subconscious. If you want your life to be more peaceful and calm, or more positive, then spend time in the company of people that are calm and positive. Listen to music, read books, watch TV shows and movies that are uplifting and positive. Give yourself positive messages daily through reading affirmations about the person you are becoming.
6. Invite a trusted group of diverse people to become accountability partners with you and give you honest reactions to your thinking and your behavior. Regularly share with them what you are thinking or planning to do and ask them individually for their reactions.
7. Write down in detail over several days how you think you come across. Write out the characteristics, both the desirable and the undesirable ones that you think make up who you are.
8. Ask a favor of your chosen group of accountability partners, the people that you have given permission to confront you and tell you what they see in you. Ask each of them alone to tell you the characteristics that they see in you, both the desirable and the undesirable ones. Listen to what they say and do not try to make excuses or explain away their observations of you.

9. Compare what your accountability partners all say to see if there are similarities. If most of them say the same things, then that is probably how you are really coming across to others.
10. Compare the consensus or similarities of what others see in you with what you see in yourself. The closer your perception is to the general consensus of others, the better you are getting to know yourself. You will become increasingly able to predict new outcomes of your chosen behavior.
11. Invite other people to reflect back to you how you come across to them. You will gain a much more accurate view of yourself than just relying on your own subjective sense of who you are. By seeing yourself more objectively you discover the areas in your worldview that are causing patterns of repeated consequences and need reprogramming.

Principle Three

You Become What You Think About

Below is a collection of thoughts written down by some of history's most famous positive influencers. Dale Carnegie collected many of them during his lifetime in the early twentieth century. They were published after his death in a book titled *Dale Carnegie's Scrapbook*. The motivational speaker Earl Nightingale collected them, too, during his career in the 1950's and 1960's. He included them in his famous audio recording titled *The Strangest Secret*. Since then, other people have discovered and published the same thoughts and ideas. They hold a fascination for people that recognize the powerful truth in them.

The Probable Future

"**A man's life is what his thoughts make of it.**" *Marcus Aurelius, philosopher and Roman emperor from 161–180 A.D.*

"**A man is what he thinks about all day long.**" *Ralph Waldo Emerson, 1803–1882, American author, poet and philosopher*

"**The greatest discovery of my generation is that human beings can alter their lives by altering their attitudes of mind.**" *William James, 1842–1910, philosopher called the "Father of American Psychology"*

"**If you think in negative terms, you will get negative results; if you think in positive terms, you will get positive results.**" *Norman Vincent Peale, 1898–1993, Christian pastor, author of "The Power of Positive Thinking", founder and editor of "Guideposts" magazine*

"**There is nothing either good or bad, but thinking makes it so.**" *(Hamlet) William Shakespeare, 1564–1616, English playwright and poet*

"**All that a man achieves and all that he fails to achieve is the direct result of his own thoughts.**" *James Allen, 1864–1912, English philosopher and author of "As a Man Thinketh"*

You Become What You Think About

"**We have free will, but our free will lies in our choice of thoughts.**" *Emmet Fox, 1886–1951, British theologian, philosopher and author who influenced early members of Alcoholics Anonymous in the USA*

"**All that we are is the result of what we have thought.**" *Gautama Buddha, 563–483 B.C., royal Nepalese prince who gave up his wealth to pursue enlightenment and fathered Buddhism*

"**As a man thinketh in his heart, so is he.**" *King Solomon in Proverbs 23:7 of The Holy Bible (King James Version)*

"**The world we have created is a product of our own thinking. It cannot be changed without changing our thinking.**" *Albert Einstein, 1879–1955, German born mathematician and theoretical physicist, won Nobel Prize for Physics in 1921, developed Theory of Relativity*

"**It's not what happens to you, but how you react to it that matters.**" *Epictetus, 55–135 A.D., Greek-born Roman slave, later freed, Stoic philosopher and writer*

"**Two men looked out through prison bars; one saw mud, the other saw stars.**" *Anonymous*

The Probable Future

"How we think shows through in how we act. Attitudes are mirrors of the mind. They reflect thinking." *David J. Schwartz, American author of "The Magic of Thinking Big", published in 1959*

"We become what we think about." *Earl Nightingale, 1921–1989, high school dropout who became inspirational author and motivational speaker with popular radio and TV shows*

"Adopting the right attitude can convert a negative stress into a positive one." *Hans Selye, MD, 1907–1982, Canadian doctor who first identified stress-related disease*

"A man is but the product of his thoughts. What he thinks, he becomes." *Mahatma Gandhi, 1869–1948, political and spiritual leader of India's struggle for independence from British rule through non-violent resistance*

"... as you think, so you will be." *Dale Carnegie, 1888–1955, American author and developer of courses in self-improvement, leadership, public speaking, interpersonal skills and salesmanship, wrote "How to Win Friends and Influence People"*

Many great thinkers down through the centuries from different countries, cultures and religions have arrived at the same conclusion. Perhaps Earl

Nightingale said it best, "We become what we think about."

> **What you think about becomes the messages that shape your worldview.**
>
> — *Don Osborne*

If the messages that seep into your subconscious and shape your worldview include the notion that there is only one way to see and do certain things, then you will develop "all or nothing" thinking. That limits your ability to be creative or find solutions to problems. Open-mindedness does not have to compromise your belief systems. Intellectually and emotionally secure people can maintain their core beliefs and values while examining other points of view and seeking a broader understanding of the world and how it works.

The beliefs within your worldview are the foundation upon which your thinking is based. Have you ever found yourself strongly opposed to the views of other people and wonder, "How can anyone think that way?" It may be that your thinking and their thinking are both logical, but based on different foundational beliefs. An analogy is Base 8 math versus Base 10 math. In the western world, we use Base 10 math. When writing a number with two or more digits, the digit to the far right is the number of ones, up to the number nine. The next number to the left of the ones represents tens. So, when you write "36" the number represents three tens and six ones. In a Base 8 math system, the digits on the right are ones up to the number seven. The next number to the left, instead of representing how many tens, represents how many eights are in the number. Using the same number 36 as an example, in a Base 8 system, there are six ones and three eights. When counting the number of items that the numbers represent, in a Base 10 system, 36 equals three tens and six ones which equals 36 ones. In a Base 8 system, 36 equals three eights and six ones, and that equals 30 ones. Consequently, when a Base 10 thinker disagrees with a Base 8 thinker about the value of the number 36, it may be that the thinking processes are logical for both parties. They are just basing their thinking on different foundations. A Base 10 thinker does not have to stop being a Base 10 thinker in order to understand a Base 8 thinker. You must, however, find out from the person with whom you disagree just what their foundational beliefs are. You can discover why they think as they do. You might still disagree, but you can understand them. Then you can better predict their choices and behavior. It won't be like yours. One of the common tragic mistakes that American government foreign policy leaders make is expecting people from other cultures with vastly different worldviews to think and behave the same way that Americans do.

Another common block to functioning is self-centeredness. When you are thinking mostly about yourself, you become less able to think about others or to problem solve. Self-centeredness is not just the conceit that may come to mind when the term is used. People with very low self-esteem are terribly self-centered, as well. They just think about how inadequate or worthless they are instead of how superior and brilliant or good-looking they are. Both are thinking mostly about themselves. That interferes with their ability to think more objectively about problems that need to be addressed. They have difficulty successfully engaging with other people in meaningful relationships.

People Who Defeat Themselves and People Who Excel

Perhaps you have heard the old saying, "If you continue to do what you've always done, you will continue to get what you've always gotten." The obvious lesson is that if you don't like the patterns in your life, then you must make changes. Remember that your behavior stems from choices that you make. Your choices are based on your values and beliefs about how the world functions. It does not matter whether your beliefs about yourself and your circumstances are accurate or not. To you, your beliefs are your reality. There is an objective reality that is independent of your perceptions and your beliefs. Your understanding of reality, however, is always filtered through the subjective lens of your worldview. That is where your beliefs about the world around you reside. Ultimately, you make choices and act as a result of those beliefs.

Maybe you have encountered people with handicaps or challenges that feel depressed and overcome by their circumstances. They give up on trying to succeed at anything. Perhaps you have also met people with the same kinds of handicaps or challenges that have very positive outlooks on life. They set goals or have interests outside of themselves and get on with life. What makes people react so differently to the same challenges that life has dealt them?

> "Whether you think you can, or you think you can't, you're right."
>
> — *Henry Ford*

Have you ever wondered why some people always seem to have "bad luck", and others seem to experience good fortune every time they turn around?

You Become What You Think About

Have you ever thought of the fact that every man and woman is a "self-made man" or "self-made woman" but only the successful ones will admit it? Many people, it seems, would rather blame circumstances or other people for repeated consequences in their lives. These folks are externally oriented. They see their problems as originating outside of themselves. They therefore also see the solutions to their problems as needing to come from outside of themselves. They may try to manipulate others into solving their problems for them. When no one rescues them from their problems, externally oriented people view themselves as victims and blame others. They go through life complaining that they are the victims of circumstances or the mistreatment of other people for which they have no responsibility. Sadly, externally oriented people are really the victims of their own thinking. They often say things like "I had no choice" when explaining why they did something. They do not realize that they have a wide variety of choices.

Their functionally negative worldview results in their choosing to do and say things that are self-defeating. Then they interpret the negative consequences of their own behavior through the lens of that same faulty worldview, and see themselves as victims.

By contrast, some folks tend to *not* do things that are self-defeating. Instead, they are aware that they have choices. They choose to do and say things that result in positive outcomes. These people tend to learn from their mistakes, correct them, and usually do not repeat them. People in this category are internally oriented and see their problems as being caused by their own chosen behavior that results from their own thinking (worldview). They examine their own thinking and are adaptable enough to make changes in the choices that they make. Anyone is capable of enjoying a productive and happy life, despite setbacks and losses, by making decisions based on a functionally positive worldview.

From the 1940's until the 1960's, a psychiatrist in New York City named Dr. Harry Tiebout focused his professional work on alcoholics. Dr. Tiebout described the differences between alcoholics who were still caught up in negative thinking, and those who underwent some "conversion" process and achieved sobriety through a very different way of thinking. The "negative" thinkers were described by Dr. Tiebout as people who were "at odds with the world", loners who were self-centered, demanding, and often angry that things did not go their way. According to Dr. Tiebout, these people blamed circumstances and other people for the unpleasant consequences they experienced. They didn't recover from alcoholism as long as they thought that way. However, Dr. Tiebout described the recovering, sober alcoholics he observed as emotionally healthier than normal non-alcoholic people. Their thinking changed to a "positive" view and the individuals saw themselves as part of a greater whole. They expressed feelings of connectedness, and a "live and let live" attitude. These recovering alcoholics had a joy for living, and an acceptance of personal responsibility. Dr. Tiebout documented his observations of thousands of alcoholics with whom he worked. He described some miraculous changes as people's worldviews changed.

In Dr. Maxwell Maltz's classic book *Psychocybernetics*, he illustrates the point with observations from his career as a plastic surgeon. Dr. Maltz described correcting facial disfigurements that resulted in people seeing themselves differently. They then developed much more positive outlooks on life. One fellow that had avoided other people out of embarrassment changed and became a successful sales professional after surgery. There were, however, cases where plastic surgery corrected the outer defect, but the individual still saw themselves as disfigured. Their image of themselves did not change in their worldview, and as a result, their thinking did not change. They still avoided people and saw themselves as unacceptable.

The key, Dr. Maltz pointed out, is not how you see yourself on the outside. It is how you see yourself deep in your self-image that determines your choices and behavior.

Dr. William Glasser is another famous psychiatrist and the author of *Reality Therapy*. He helped start a trend in counseling called "cognitive behavioral therapy" that is still very popular. Dr. Glasser disputed the popular medical perspective that "mentally ill" people suffer from a disease. Instead, Dr. Glasser suggested that such people are "failures" in life because they do not accept responsibility for themselves. If you plan and, with support, change your behavior, your feelings will change in the process. Therefore, if you are depressed, talking about how depressed you are with a therapist will simply reinforce how depressed you feel. Instead, if you change your behavior to something that is upbeat, or at least gets you thinking about something other than yourself, your feelings will be less depressed and your mood will improve. The following is an actual case.

A Case Study

Several years ago, a young woman, then in her early twenties, began seeing me for counseling. I will refer to her here as Wanda. Wanda grew up in a home with a father who was successful professionally, but who was also a violent alcoholic. At home, he would beat Wanda's mother with his fists, often yanking her hair out by the handful. Once he pushed her down a flight of stairs. Wanda witnessed this horror repeatedly for years while growing up, and lived in fear for her mother's life. The community did not know that the successful professional was a raging violent alcoholic. He should have been jailed for repeatedly assaulting his wife, and nearly killing her. As a young teenager, Wanda began experimenting with alcohol and other drugs, perhaps partly to escape from the terror at home. Her teenage boyfriend died in an accident, and Wanda became even more depressed. She overdosed on sedatives and alcohol on more than one occasion and was hospitalized each time. Her depression was obvious, and her overdoses were interpreted as suicide attempts. A psychiatrist misdiagnosed her as schizophrenic when he saw her under the influence of a variety of street drugs. As a result, Wanda was placed in a psychiatric hospital for nearly a year. She was treated with a number of medications intended for schizophrenics. When she was released, she was shifted from one outpatient counselor to another. They all focused their discussions with her on how depressed and suicidal she was. I was her seventh counselor in three years.

During our first session together, I asked Wanda what she did. She replied that she was depressed. I told her that I did not want to talk with her about how she felt. I wanted to know what her daily routine activities were. It took Wanda a moment to grasp that I was unwilling to discuss her depression. Finally, she was able to tell me that she spent most days alone in her apartment. She read horror novels with the blinds drawn, and avoided interaction with anyone. At night she was terrified, and repeatedly looked under her bed to see if anyone was there that might hurt her. She continued to smoke marijuana whenever she could get it, which made her more paranoid. She passed her evenings watching "slasher" movies at home – horror movies with explicit scenes of people being murdered in the goriest methods. I agreed to be Wanda's counselor on two conditions. She had to quit smoking marijuana, and we would **not** meet in my office in a community mental health center where she was used to seeing therapists.

Our next session was held at the local city park. We walked and talked about activities that Wanda enjoyed earlier in her life. She said that she liked to play softball when she was younger. As time went by, and she began to trust me, I used my influence with her to get her to join a co-ed adult softball league in the city. She played catcher throughout the summer, and began making friends within the softball league. Gradually, I was able to influence Wanda to give up horror movies and books. She began engaging in activities that took her out of constantly thinking about herself. She loved animals, so, with encouragement, Wanda looked for work taking care of pets at a veterinarian's office. Before long, Wanda met a young man in a support group that she attended, and fell in love. I had the pleasure of attending her wedding, and she was not at all depressed that day.

Over a period of about eighteen months, Wanda's mood changed dramatically because her behavior changed dramatically. As her mood lifted, together we were able to help Wanda re-frame her interpretation of events in her childhood. As a result, her worldview began to change. As she experienced new positive people and events, her worldview changed even more. Though she had no choice in how her life started out, she began gradually to accept responsibility for the direction that the rest of her life would take. Wanda began reprogramming her thinking with positive input from her new environment. It became evident that she was not schizophrenic, and she did not have a condition over which she was helpless.

You Become What You Think About

Key Points & Action You Can Take

Your behavior and the outcome of your life results from what you repeatedly think about. You can choose what you think about and thereby alter your worldview and the choices that you make.

1. You can change your probable future by changing the way that you think. In order to change your behavior long-term, and, therefore, the outcomes in your life, you must ultimately change your thinking patterns.
2. By changing the way that you think, your worldview will be altered. This usually occurs through some break through, or epiphany, an "a ha" experience. That moment of clarity must be followed by continuing to change the messages that you allow into your mind (reprogramming). Breakthroughs may occur suddenly as a catharsis, or slowly over time as a dawning awareness.
3. In order to manage the messages entering your mind, you may have to change your environment, or your relationships. Some environments or people may be toxic to you.
4. Feelings, which influence and sometimes overwhelm thoughts, can be changed short term by changing patterns of behavior. Likewise, your thoughts can be changed short term by altering a behavior pattern. In order for the change in

your behavior to become permanent, however, thinking (worldview) must change.

5. Once you change the way that you think, and are strong enough to withstand negative messages, you can influence others to change the ways that they think. You can thereby impact families, groups or whole organizations.
6. Your thinking must undergo constant examination and reprogramming. Continue to upgrade your thinking with the positive influences you choose. Otherwise, it will revert to the original programming.
7. The better you know yourself the more accurately you can predict what will probably happen in your future. You will better understand how you think and the choices you probably will make in the future.
8. It is possible to detect a person's or group of people's worldview by the things that they say and do over time. Patterns of behavior reflect people's thinking. By understanding how people think and what their worldview is, it's possible to predict how they are likely to act and the choices that they will probably make.

Principle Four

The Only Four Ways That You Interact With Others

When Andy acted up in our class in grade school, the teacher made him sit on a stool in a front corner of the room. The teacher thought that she was punishing him and that he would stop acting out. Andy giggled and continued to disrupt the class as we students focused on him and not on the teacher's lesson. Andy's misbehavior was probably a ploy to gain attention, and he certainly got it. In fact, the teacher actually rewarded Andy's bad behavior in class by making him a spectacle, thereby giving him more attention. The teacher inadvertently provided **positive reinforcement** for the boy's disruptive behavior. That increased the likelihood that he would act out again later on, and he did.

The Probable Future

Whether rearing a child or working with a team of professionals in a billion dollar enterprise, every human interaction involves either giving or taking away something. Everything that you give or take away is either pleasant or unpleasant to the other person or group. It has an impact on what the other person or group does. This is behavioral psychology's principle of operant conditioning. It has been repeatedly shown to be true through experiments and field tests. You can predict people's behavior using this principle. If you understand it, then you can intentionally influence what people will do.

Behavioral psychologists have shown that there are four primary ways that we interact with each other.

	Pleasant	**Unpleasant**
Giving	1 **Reward** (Positive Reinforcement) **Rewarded Behavior Increases**	2 **Punishment** (Punishment) **Punished Behavior Decreases Slightly But Deceit Increases**
Taking Away	3 **Punishment** (Extinction) **Punished Behavior Decreases**	4 **Reward** (Negative Reinforcement) **Rewarded Behavior Increases**

The Only Four Ways That You Interact With Others

The Need for Approval

Ask a roomful of folks "How many of you receive too much approval or appreciation for what you do?" Not a soul will raise their hand and you will hear chuckles at such a silly question. Our culture is not based on appreciating or approving each other. More often, you'll hear the comment, "No matter what I do it never seems to be good enough." The speaker may be talking about a parent when growing up, a spouse, or a work supervisor, but it is a common sentiment. It is easy to understand why so many people suffer from low self-esteem. Even the people who appear to be very successful on the outside with fame and fortune sometimes talk about self-doubt and even self-loathing. Their experiences, perhaps early in life, did not include enough positive messages. And as adults, we still crave the appreciation that we deserve just for being *who* we are.

If you give someone something that he considers pleasant for something that he did, he is very likely to do it again. That is a reward and psychologists call it "positive reinforcement". The reward "reinforces" the behavior and it's "positive" because you are giving something as opposed to taking something away. The reward might be money, a dozen roses, a gold star for a child, a word of praise, or whatever the person or group values. Many adults value greater independence at work and a sense of purpose more highly than monetary bonuses. It must, however, be something that the recipient wants. As a result, the person receiving the reward tends to repeat the behavior that is rewarded. The reward must be intentional, and there must be a connection between the reward and the behavior. (See quadrant 1 in the diagram.)

	Pleasant	Unpleasant
Giving	1 **Reward** (Positive Reinforcement) **Rewarded Behavior Increases** ↑	
Taking Away		

The Recipient's Perspective

While referring to Jesus' admonition to "Do to others as you would have them do to you," Dr. Clay Smith, a Christian pastor, suggests that we also "Do to others as *others* would want us to do to them." The emphasis is on seeing things from the other person's viewpoint.

The Only Four Ways That You Interact With Others

A division leader at a firm where I was consulting complained that rewarding productivity didn't really work. When I asked her to explain, she told me that a group of sixty people in her division brought a project together ahead of time and under budget. As a reward, she gave each person flowers and candy. "But," she said, "they didn't all appreciate it." I asked her how many of the people that worked on the project were men. She said, "About half." I suggested to her that the men that worked on the project might have preferred tickets to a ball game or something else that appealed to them. The division leader said, "Well, I like flowers and candy, but I never thought that everyone else wouldn't appreciate them." That was the point. You must analyze rewards from the perspective of the individual or group that is being rewarded. In getting to know co-workers, subordinates, friends and family-members, ask about the kinds of things that they value or enjoy. That way you will learn what **they** consider as rewards.

By intentionally rewarding specific behaviors, parents, teachers, work supervisors, and spouses can encourage action which then becomes predictable. When I got home several hours before my wife one afternoon, I fixed her favorite dinner, set the table with candlelight and put on her favorite music. After dinner, I cleaned up the kitchen and did the dishes. She rewarded me with affection, which greatly increased the likelihood that I would do that again.

The Probable Future

Several companies in the same field hold the view that employees are already being paid for doing their jobs and don't need additional rewards. The management of each company believes that if employees get to keep their jobs then that is their reward. Employees do not feel appreciated. They feel like they are just numbers to their managers. Absenteeism and turnover are high while morale is low. The companies are constantly having to recruit and train replacements. By the time new employees become really proficient at their jobs, they leave because of the negative environment. Productivity remains low.

By contrast, the owner of a smaller competing company has developed a very loyal and industrious workforce. He focuses on rewarding employees' performance. By regularly visiting each division, he knows most of his employees by name. He makes it a point to visit briefly with each individual. He asks about their families and what they enjoy doing when they aren't at work. The business owner keeps a file of what he discovers about each person. He is particularly interested in finding out what different people consider as rewards. For example, he learned that Ricardo loves fishing and participates in bass tournaments whenever possible. Belinda, a single parent, likes to take her two children to a nearby Six Flags theme park. Some respond to getting an extra half-day off to golf or be with their families. Others appreciate his praise in front of their peers with a plaque or a certificate. Still others want monetary bonuses. The smart business owner contracts with his employees in a leadership style called "Transactional Leadership." He tells a group, a division or a team leader what production level, quality level or deadline they need to meet for a specific customer. Nearly every time, his employees exceed his expectations. The business owner delights in handing out the rewards that each person values most... tickets to Six Flags or to the next bass tournament, a $100 bill, etc. He is able to keep experienced employees and has very little turnover. Absenteeism is practically non-existent. His employees are willing to exert extra effort because they know it is appreciated. People enjoy coming to work and morale is high. Even though the company is smaller, they outperform all of their competitors by more than 15% every year. The owner says that the expense of giving rewards for performance is far outweighed by the increased performance and profitability.

Punishment

By giving something unpleasant, you punish people for their behavior. (See quadrant 2 in the diagram.) Again, the punishment is from the viewpoint of the person receiving it. If a work supervisor harshly criticizes a subordinate in front of her peers, she may feel humiliated. The unpleasantness may be interpreted as a punishment.

	Pleasant	Unpleasant
Giving		2 **Punishment** (Punishment) **Punished Behavior Decreases Slightly But Deceit Increases** ↓
Taking Away		

> Contrary to what many people apparently believe, punishment does not improve performance.
>
> — *Don Osborne*

The Only Four Ways That You Interact With Others

The person being punished may slightly change their behavior for a while but she will become resentful. The behavior may even continue out of spite for the punishment. Deceit and distrust almost certainly develop. The person may not perform the punished behavior as often, but may do it when the punisher is not watching. Children who are punished as a primary way of managing their behavior often will start telling lies in order to avoid further punishment. Then they usually develop deceitful ways of getting around rules.

Once, a parent asked me how she could vent her anger at her child if she didn't punish him by hitting him, calling him names, or yelling and screaming at him. She didn't realize that handling her own anger and changing her child's behavior were two separate issues.

The new CEO of a health care facility frequently displayed his temper in front of the administrative staff. He threw their paperwork across the room when he discovered an error. He seemed not to care that he was creating enormous resentment. The female employees often cried and everyone began hating to come to work. Their boss's bullying behavior was viewed as punishment for not being perfect. The CEO declared that he would "teach" the employees not to ever make mistakes while working for him. His administrative staff began quitting. Each time that a long-term employee resigned, she took with her the knowledge of how to solve problems that were common for that organization. As most of the administrative workforce left, their replacements did not have the experience with the company's recurring issues. When the experienced employees were gone, their replacements didn't know how to solve those problems. Soon the efficiency was so low that the company functioned from crisis to crisis. The CEO blamed the employees for poor performance.

An Effective Way to Correct Behavior

At the age of fifteen, David was an excellent student in high school with a raging desire to play guitar in a rock band. Given a guitar and small amplifier for Christmas, he practiced for hours on end every day. An agreement was reached between David and his parents that his daily guitar practice was acceptable as long as his grades did not drop. The arrangement was, if his grades dropped during any grading period, he would lose guitar-playing privileges during the week so that he could concentrate on his studies. He would be allowed to play the guitar only on the weekends until the next grading period showed his grades were back up to the high standard that was expected. Sure enough, his grades dropped one grading period. The agreed-upon arrangement was immediately enforced without further discussion. Removing David's guitar playing privilege was a pre-arranged, agreed-upon contract. Something that he really enjoyed was taken away as a consequence of not maintaining high

The Only Four Ways That You Interact With Others

grades. *The consequence was directly connected to the behavior that was of concern. He was still permitted to practice his guitar on the weekends. As a result, David responded to the consequence by raising his grades to a level higher than ever before for the next grading period. His parents then reinstated his guitar playing privileges throughout the week with the same agreement still in force. David's grades never dropped again, and he formed his own rock band.*

As in the case of David, taking away something that is pleasant is another form of punishment. When used properly, however, it corrects the behavior it is focused on without causing resentment. (See quadrant 3 in the diagram.)

	Pleasant	**Unpleasant**
Giving		
Taking Away	3 **Punishment** (Extinction) **Punished Behavior Decreases** ↓	

The Probable Future

The challenge for most of us is applying this form of punishment without turning it into the other punishment style in which something unpleasant is given. David's family used "Taking Away Something Pleasant" appropriately. The probable future was predicted. The family recognized the possibility that David's guitar playing might interfere with his grades. The agreement was established in advance of the problem arising. He was still permitted to play his guitar on weekends. If David's parents had waited until his grades dropped to spring the consequence on him, he would not have responded as well. If they lectured him and belittled him for failing to keep his grades up, or if they refused to let him play guitar at all, even on weekends, then the punishment would have become "Giving Something Unpleasant" instead of "Taking Away Something Pleasant". David would have become resentful and may have tried to sneak guitar playing behind his parents' backs. This form of punishment, "Taking Away Something Pleasant," is very effective when used properly and is the idea behind "grounding" kids. However, many parents quickly turn it into the less effective form of punishment of "Giving Something Unpleasant" by making the grounding last too long, or yelling at the child in the process or otherwise giving the child a reason to resent them.

The same principle can be used in the workplace. Giving employees privileges that they earn and removing the privileges if the performance level is not maintained is an excellent example. As long as the employees can earn the privileges back again, and the organization's management does not turn the removal of privileges into a humiliation, then the principle works well. Manipulation and resentment are avoided by discussing up front what the expectations are, and with everyone agreeing on the arrangement. This is another example of a very effective leadership style called *Transactional Leadership*.

Rewarding by Removing Something Unpleasant

I saw a humorous saying on the internet that parodies misguided management practices. It said, "The beatings will continue until morale improves." Actually, the humor reflects a twist on the fourth quadrant of the behavioral grid. Taking away something that is unpleasant is a kind of reward. Behavioral psychologists call this "negative reinforcement". It's "reinforcement" because the behavior being focused on is rewarded, and "negative" because something is being taken away or subtracted.

The Probable Future

	Pleasant	**Unpleasant**
Giving		
Taking Away		4 Reward (Negative Reinforcement) **Rewarded Behavior Increases**

An executive sales professional was very good at his primary responsibility of selling his company's services and bringing in new business. He absolutely despised the paperwork that accompanied every sale, however. He made lots of detail mistakes when he did it. If he took a test like the Herrmann Brain Dominance test, it might have shown that the sales pro was "wired" for selling and definitely was handicapped when it came to detail-oriented tasks like paperwork. He put off doing all of the paperwork until he was in trouble with senior management. Drudging through the paperwork took away from his selling time and was so tedious for him that his sales productivity was in jeopardy. The salesman's immediate supervisor was smart. He figured out how much money was being lost as the super salesman was slowly doing the paperwork that he hated so much, and his attitude was being negatively affected. Then the supervisor made a deal with his star salesman. One of the younger salesmen new to the company was a whiz at paperwork and details. However, he did not yet have the confidence or skills necessary to be a top producer. The supervisor arranged for the new salesman to do the paperwork for the old pro in exchange for the old pro mentoring the young newcomer. Together they made a terrific team, and as a result, the executive salesman's productivity soared. Something that was very unpleasant...paperwork...was taken away and the senior sales professional interpreted that as a reward for bringing in more business to his company. He felt in greater control of his professional life and he was able to do more of what he did well. As an added benefit, the younger salesman accompanied the old pro on sales calls and learned the skills necessary to become a successful sales professional in his own right. The sales manager was indeed clever.

Analyzation, Application and Effectiveness

Understanding and applying the principles of the operant conditioning behavior grid will give you great insight into how people respond to rewards and punishments. Whether or not you are aware of it, every interaction that you have with people fits into one of the grid's quadrants. You are continually rewarding and punishing the people in your life. How much more effective can you be if you begin examining your interactions with the people around you? You become aware of behavioral patterns and why they occur. Soon, you can predict what is going to happen because you recognize the way that we all reward and punish each other. You can then intentionally change the way that you interact with the people in your life at work, in your social circles and at home. The result will be a very predictable change in the way that people respond to you.

The single most effective interaction for changing behavior is positive reinforcement, where something pleasant is given to an individual or group for something that they did. It greatly increases the likelihood that they will do it again. The least effective interaction is the sort of punishment where something unpleasant is given. Not only is that form of punishment the least effective in changing behavior, it increases resentment and deceit. People won't like you, won't want to be around you or work for you, and they're more likely to lie to you.

By combining positive and negative reinforcement, it becomes very easy to shape or mold behavior into what is most desirable. Contract in advance with the people you wish to influence so that the interaction is understood and agreed upon by everyone involved. If certain actions are performed, a desirable reward will be given to the person or group. The reward may be to give something desirable, or to remove something undesirable. Studies around the world have shown that increased autonomy or

The Only Four Ways That You Interact With Others

independence and meaningfulness in the workplace are more rewarding for most adults than monetary bonuses. When the agreement is understood, then the desired behavior is extremely likely to be performed. This is true whether you are dealing with a work team or individual at work, or a child or other loved one. This way, you are not manipulating people, but influencing them according to agreed-upon arrangements.

Key Points & Action You Can Take

You interact with the people around you in four primary ways. Either you are giving something or taking something away, and the things you are giving and taking away are either pleasant or unpleasant for the recipients. You may not be aware of how you interact or come across to others. You might be rewarding the wrong behaviors and punishing people around you without realizing it.

1. If you give pleasant things, tangible or intangible, then it rewards behavior that is associated with the gift. That increases the likelihood that the behavior will be repeated.
2. If you give unpleasant things, whether physical or verbal, then it punishes the person or group for the associated behavior. The punished behavior may decrease slightly, but resentment, distrust, and deceit increase in the relationship.
3. If you take away something that is pleasant for unacceptable behavior, then the behavior being punished will decrease. Do this without expressions of anger or disappointment, but as a matter-of-fact consequence that all parties were aware of in advance. Then it does not create the resentment and deceit that occurs with the other form of punishment.
4. Taking away something unpleasant is a reward and increases the likelihood that the behavior being rewarded will be repeated. Although

effective, this reward does not have as powerful an impact as giving people something that they want.
5. Begin analyzing interactions with people according to this principle. Think about how you affect the people around you at work, in social settings and at home. How do they respond to you? Observe and analyze how other people interact and affect each other.
6. Determine which behavioral pattern(s) you use most often. Are you generally one who rewards or punishes? Share the behavior grid with others close to you and ask them to analyze how you come across. You may not be able to see yourself objectively, and you might be surprised at how you affect the people around you from their viewpoint.
7. Openly discuss rewards and punishments with the people in your life. Decide together the kinds of behavior that are most desirable in the different contexts of work, social life and family life.
8. Decide what you want to change in the way that you deal with people. Think of specific ways that you can increase your own rewarding behavior and decrease your own punishing behavior. Intentionally change your own behavior in order to change the impact that you have on others.
9. Practice analyzing people's interactions until you become accurate at predicting what will happen before it happens.

Principle Five

Systems of Relationships with Predictable Patterns

A great orchestra is composed of individual instrumentalists, but they all play the same song. The orchestra functions as a unit, a system of different components that interact together. All human beings are members of larger systems of relationships with observable patterns. You can see how different groups of people deal with leadership issues, decision-making, power, communication, and how well they adapt to change. You cannot change any one part of a system without affecting all of the other parts of the system in some way. That would be like the horn section starting to play a different

The Probable Future

tune than the rest of the orchestra. Every instrument player would hear two different songs. Either the horn section will be pressured to rejoin the rest of the orchestra, or the rest of the orchestra will change to play the song that the horn section is playing. Another option may be that the horn section is kicked out of the orchestra.

Systems tend to resist change and try to maintain a status quo or balance, called a "homeostasis". This tendency to resist change occurs even if a change is needed and desirable. People within human systems assume roles where they fit in even if the role is dysfunctional. If people leave a system and the role that they fulfilled is a part of the system's homeostasis, or normal way of operating, then someone will be pressured to move into the vacated role.

Many organizations operate as dysfunctional systems, and consistently implement the worst practices that ultimately create more problems for the business. Similarly, families are systems of relationships. Each individual in a family has a role, just as members of organizations do. Some roles serve to provide the system leadership, and some roles provide the system someone to blame for all that goes wrong. When individuals leave systems of relationships, the system will typically focus on someone else within the family or the organization to take on that role.

Systems of Relationships with Predictable Patterns

Bill was a chronic alcoholic who had spent time in prison for a crime he committed while intoxicated. His wife blamed him for everything that ever went wrong in the family. She handled the family's finances and reared the children, encouraging them to ignore their father because he was usually drunk. Due to an arrest for public intoxication, Bill wound up in a detox facility that convinced him to try Alcoholics Anonymous and counseling. Bill sobered up and found a job. He attended AA and counseling and turned his life around. Soon, he wanted to take his place in the family as husband and father, and his wife resisted. Perhaps she was afraid that Bill would relapse and go back to drinking, or maybe she could not adapt to the change in the family roles. After Bill had been sober for a year, his wife screamed at him, "I wish you would go back to drinking!" The couple divorced, but Bill's ex-wife continued to blame him for everything that went wrong for their children and her. After a couple of years, Bill was killed in an accident. I saw Bill's widow on the street a few years later and inquired as to how she was doing. She began complaining about Bill's alcoholism, and I stopped her. I said, "Bill is dead, and besides, he was sober the last few years of his life." She looked at me blankly, turned and walked away. Although the reality of Bill's life had changed, the family system he had been a part of did not. Bill's widow and the children continued as though nothing had changed. By then, the oldest son was drinking heavily and Bill's widow focused all of her attention on him, as he took his father's role in the family.

Observing this family, their every move was predictable, based on an understanding of how systems work.

If systems do not change, then the same practices, policies and outcomes continue, regardless of whether the results are healthy or destructive to the system itself.

Creativity Requires Change (and is Therefore Resisted)

In a business meeting the agenda is to solve a problem facing the company. Elizabeth proposes an idea that she thinks might help. Bob says, "That was tried in the Cleveland division last year and it didn't work." Stinging from the rebuke, Elizabeth does not offer anything further. Steve pipes up and suggests another idea that is innovative and may solve the problem. Frank retorts, "That would require that we redesign the processes that we're using now. We can't do that." Steve joins Elizabeth in remaining silent the rest of the meeting. Marianne suggests a proposal that she has been working on for several weeks. She hands out a fact sheet that she developed to support her proposal. After silently reviewing it as a group, Bob announces, "This is a good idea, but it would be way too costly to implement. We need to be creative here,

Systems of Relationships with Predictable Patterns

guys. Come on now, let's come up with a solution." No one else suggests anything further. The meeting eventually closes after everyone complains about the problem some more and another meeting is scheduled. If this sounds familiar, it is the all-too-common experience of many organizations and groups of people where innovation, creativity and real problem solving are actually discouraged because it involves change.

In another scenario, Chris was hired to manage a division of a medium-sized company that was struggling. Chris worked hard to establish rapport with everyone in the division and gain their trust. It took a while because the company was run by an executive team that shared a negative view of employees. They had created an environment of distrust and fear that permeated the entire organization. Given a little leeway to change some things in the division locally, and mandated to meet specific goals, Chris did remarkably well. She worked with her local team to improve the division's performance from seventeenth of eighteen divisions to second in the company in only six months. Eventually, even though her division made such a dramatic improvement, Chris was fired for questioning the processes of the corporate headquarters that held the organization back and created problems for her division. Chris tried to be diplomatic when raising questions about the processes that were so inefficient and offered alternative suggestions. The senior management team viewed Chris as a troublemaker though, and not a "team player". Once Chris was fired, someone more to the senior executive team's liking was promoted to be the division's new manager. Performance dropped back almost to the levels where things were when Chris was first hired. Key performers in the division quit rather than go back to the way things were.

Change and Change Management

Change management is simply gaining acceptance and cooperation in doing something differently. Creativity is the author of the need for change. The following is an example of the most successful approach to change and change management in an organization. The same principles apply to small groups, teams, and families.

> "If you don't like change, you're going to like irrelevance even less."
>
> – *General Eric Shinseki,*
> *Chief of Staff, U.S. Army*

A corporate CEO valued his employees and was aware that the work environment contributed to their productivity. He was also aware of the need for the company to become more flexible and make rapid adjustments to stay

Systems of Relationships with Predictable Patterns

competitive in their market. Rather than make decisions by himself and issue edicts from his office, he met first with his division heads about changes that the organization needed to make. He asked for their input on how the organization might best improve its structure and processes. The CEO was concerned that his company not suffer from "strategic myopia". That is when management fails to recognize changes that are occurring because they hold strong beliefs about the way things are and don't seek input outside of themselves. So, the CEO then arranged to meet with each division separately. He and each division's head met first with the department managers in the division. They were asked for their view of what adjustments and changes were necessary in order for the company to thrive. Next, the CEO, the division head and the managers met with the line staff and asked for their input. The CEO repeated this process with each division until everyone in the entire company understood that changes needed to be made and why. Everyone had a chance to tell him what they recommended. As a result, the CEO and his senior management team had the perspective of everyone in the company within thirty days. The employees felt as though their views mattered and they were prepared for the coming changes. As the CEO and his senior management team planned out the specific changes that needed to be made, there was almost no resistance from anyone in the organization. After the initial round of changes were in place, the CEO sent out a questionnaire requesting feedback from everyone in his company. He asked how well the changes were working and what unforeseen challenges had occurred.

As the company grew, the CEO repeated the whole process whenever there were major change initiatives that needed to be implemented. As a result, the organization grew rapidly. Staff felt valued and were willing to invest extra effort to make changes smoothly. The company thrived and people that worked there didn't want to leave. The company's reputation was excellent. People in the community eagerly sought chances to work there. The environment was a friendly cooperative workplace, and divisions collaborated rather than create silos. The CEO and his senior management team understood how systems operate and capitalized on their knowledge of very predictable patterns within organizations. They intentionally created an "open" rather than a "closed" system in their company.

Open and Closed Human Systems

Human systems are labeled as "open" or "closed" to describe differences in how groups of people function together. At question is how power is wielded and who has it. There are always concerns about rules and reactions to innovation and differences of opinion. The real issue about whether a system is open or closed is in how the product or service is provided. Can the system adapt to change? How effective is the leadership? Do people in the system cooperate and work together? Do people stay in the system or is there a high turnover? Below is a comparison of open and closed systems.

Systems of Relationships with Predictable Patterns

Closed Systems	Open Systems
1. Provide for little or no change	1. Provide for the system to change
2. Depend on rigid rules determined by whoever has the power	2. Offer choices & depend on successfully addressing real issues
3. Operate through psychological and/or physical force	3. Operate through mutual respect
4. Suspicion & fear exist about the system examining itself	4. There is a willingness for the system to examine itself
5. Some rules are covert (unspoken) & change must conform to them	5. All rules are overt (published), up-to-date, & change as needed
6. Communication is indirect, unclear, unspecific & incongruent	6. Communication is direct, clear, specific & congruent
7. Individuals' self-worth is low & people look outside the system for support	7. Individuals' self-worth is high & confidence increases; system members support each other
8. You can't talk about some things	8. Full freedom to comment on or ask about anything

The outcomes of a closed system are usually chaotic, accidental, may be inappropriate, and are, at times, destructive. The outcomes or results of an open system's purpose are related to reality and are constructive. Creativity and innovation are fostered only in open systems.

Human systems are based on beliefs and values that determine largely whether the system operates as an open or a closed system. Below is a comparison of the beliefs and values of open and closed human systems.

Closed System's Beliefs & Values	Open System's Beliefs & Values
• People cannot be trusted & must be controlled	• People will do the right thing if empowered
• Relationships have to be regulated	• Differences are natural & provide opportunities for greater understanding
• There is one right way & the one with power has it	• Mutual collaboration creates buy-in & shared accountability for outcomes
• There is always someone who knows what is best for you	• Self-determination and collective consensus building is highly valued
• Self-worth is secondary to power & performance	• Self-worth is primary and power and performance stem from it

Systems of Relationships with Predictable Patterns

In Douglas McGregor's classic book *The Human Side of Enterprise*, he developed a philosophical view of humankind. He described "Theory X" and "Theory Y" as two opposing ways that people view human behavior at work and in organizational life. McGregor felt that companies usually follow either one approach or the other. Supervisors and corporate executives can be readily categorized as Theory X or Theory Y managers by the way that they treat employees.

Theory X Assumptions

- People dislike work and will avoid it whenever possible.
- People must be coerced, controlled, directed, or threatened with punishment in order to get them to achieve an organization's objectives.
- People prefer to be directed, do not want responsibility, and have little or no ambition.
- People seek security above all else.

Note that with Theory X assumptions, management's role is to coerce and control employees. Micro-managing is justified as a way of insuring that everyone does their job. ***It is obvious that Theory X people subscribe to the beliefs and values that create closed systems.*** As a result, they create environments where people function poorly and people usually cannot wait to leave.

Theory Y Assumptions

- Work is as natural as play and rest.
- People are not lazy and will direct themselves if they are committed to the objectives.
- Appropriate rewards for achieving objectives directly influences people's commitment to achieving them.
- People learn to accept and seek responsibility.
- Anyone can be creative, have ingenuity, and be imaginative. People are capable of using these abilities to solve organizational problems.
- People have potential.

Note that with Theory Y assumptions, management's role is to develop the potential in employees. Managers encourage employees to use innovation and creativity to solve problems and achieve common goals. Theory Y managers view their employees as partners with different roles. Management believes that employees want to do a good job if given the opportunity to prove themselves. **Theory Y assumptions parallel the beliefs and values of open systems.** This worldview is an essential foundation of *Transformational Leadership*. The same principles apply whether we are observing a large organization, a division within a corporation, a church group, athletic team, or a family.

Systems of Relationships with Predictable Patterns

A controlling father did not change or adapt rules for his children as they grew older. When they were pre-schoolers, he set their bed time for 8:00 PM. However, when the older children grew up to be teenagers, he still insisted that they go to bed at 8:00 PM along with the younger kids. You can imagine the rebellion and resentment that his rigidity caused. Other family rules and expectations were just as rigid and inappropriate. He did not adapt the rules to fit the changes in his children's needs as they grew up. Some people in positions of authority over others create enormous problems for themselves and the human system for which they are responsible. This man's children left home as soon as they were legally able and his wife eventually divorced him.

The parents of another family encouraged their kids to become adults. They set clear expectations that changed as the children grew older. With each new stage of development, the children assumed greater responsibility for chores and for themselves. The older they got, the more maturely they were treated by their parents. As a result, by the time they each graduated from high school, they were prepared to take their places in the world of adulthood. The family system adapted to their needs as the kids grew up. The children became adults with a clear sense of responsibility and assumed their positions in the world and in their family as equals with their parents.

Key Points & Action You Can Take

A great orchestra is made up of individual instrumentalists, but they all play the same song. You are a member of more than one system of relationships. Systems are governed by observable patterns of rule setting, leadership, decision-making, self-examination, power, communication, core values, and the maintenance of a status quo or balance called a homeostasis. These determine how the system views and adapts to change.

1. Organizations of all kinds and sizes are observable systems. They usually have sub-systems within them which do not vary significantly from the larger system's style of functioning.
2. If a sub-system, like an individual or a division within a corporation acts very differently from the rest of the family, group or company, it will disrupt the homeostasis or balance of the whole system. If the organization as a whole operates as a closed system, then the disruptive influence, which could be you, will be pressured to conform to expectations, or will be thrown out. If the organization as a whole operates as an open system, then the disruptive influence will be evaluated for its value and the whole system may embrace the difference and change the larger system's processes.
3. Many businesses, groups and families operate as dysfunctional closed systems. They

Systems of Relationships with Predictable Patterns

consistently use the worst practices that ultimately create more problems. Some organizations, families and groups create open systems that make it possible for people to thrive and, as a result, the organizations, groups and families thrive.

4. Families, groups and organizations can and should examine their collective attitudes, knowledge base, skill levels, behaviors and activity levels, and the desired results of their work. By doing so, the most desirable results can be intentionally reached. A willingness to examine the way that the system functions, however, usually only occurs in an open system.

5. Closed human systems result from the influence of people with a worldview based on Theory X assumptions. Open human systems result from the influence of people with a worldview based on Theory Y assumptions. Again, you can observe the behavior of people and analyze their worldview, which stems from their beliefs.

6. The overall functioning of a human system becomes predictable as you observe whether it is an open or closed system. You can see whether creativity is encouraged, whether people are fearful or happy in the system, whether people are committed to the system or want to leave it.

7. You can predict with considerable accuracy how people will behave within family systems, groups, and at work, and the probable impact

that their actions will have on the system as a whole.
8. Change is always an issue with any group of people. People seem to naturally resist change because it disrupts the routine to which they have become accustomed, even if it is a dysfunctional routine and the change will be an improvement.
9. Closed systems resist change the most and do not have processes in place to accommodate necessary changes. Innovation is discouraged even though lip service is paid to the desirability of creativity.
10. Open systems recognize that change is inevitable, even if it is uncomfortable to make changes. As a result, open systems set up processes to engage everyone that will be involved or affected by the change. Open systems embrace changes as ways to become better. Innovation is highly valued and encouraged to plan specific changes in advance rather than waiting for crises to dictate the changes.
11. What sort of system did you grow up in? What sort of system do you work in? What can you do about it? Are you willing to change and exert influence to get others in the system to make appropriate changes? Should you leave the system?

Principle Six

The Patterns in Developmental Stages

When he was perhaps four years old, I tried to teach our son how to play checkers. We got down on the floor together on opposite sides of the checkerboard. I showed him how to move from one square to another, and when there was an open square behind one of my checkers, I told him to jump me. He asked, "What Daddy?" and I said, "Jump me." He crouched down, and the next thing I knew I had a laughing four year old on top of me on the floor. "I like this game, Daddy!" Fours year olds take things literally. As he grew up, he naturally developed new ways of thinking as he developed through the stages of life.

The Probable Future

Individuals, groups and organizations all undergo stages of development that are so regular that they are very predictable. For example, if you listen to a group of mothers comparing notes, you will hear them agree pretty much about when to expect children to start walking and talking, and when they are likely to respond to potty training. It is extremely important that parents understand the stages their children undergo so that expectations are realistic. An uninformed new mother may become very frustrated and even angry with her child who will not wait to relieve himself in the toilet. However, children don't develop control of their sphincter muscles until about two years of age, give or take a couple of months. Children are therefore unable to control elimination functions until then. Trying to toilet train children before they develop control over their sphincter muscles is obviously inappropriate. It is expecting a child to do what he or she is physically incapable of doing.

Puberty is also pretty predictable, give or take a year. It's pretty predictable about when grey hair will start to show up and waists will start to thicken, too. In fact, throughout the entire human life cycle, you know pretty much what to expect physically, but there are other stages that you will face.

Work groups, churches, businesses, athletic teams, families, corporations and just about every other collection of human beings undergo developmental stages. Knowing the stages that people, groups and organizations will naturally

The Patterns in Developmental Stages

face prepares you for what to expect and for how to respond.

Human Development

Sigmund Freud conceptualized human development from his own perspective that was centered on sexuality. That may say more about Freud that it does about the rest of us. He noted, however, that for a few years prior to puberty and developing an interest in the opposite sex, children typically prefer to play and be with other children of their own gender. Freud interpreted and labeled that stage of childhood development as latency or latent homosexuality. Freud suggested that adult homosexuals are people that are stuck in the latency stage of development. They have just never matured to the next stage of heterosexual interest, or they have regressed back to the latency stage as adults. Whether you agree with Freud's perspective or not, he was one of the pioneers who viewed life as a series of stages through which we all must grow.

Jean Piaget studied the learning process and how the human brain appears to gather, sort and use information in childhood and adolescence. Piaget's research broadly describes cognitive or reasoning abilities that develop in stages that are roughly similar to stages of development in other areas of your life. According to Piaget, for example, a common mistake parents make is to expect an eight or nine

The Probable Future

year old to reason like an adult. It isn't possible for the child to do so because their reasoning ability doesn't reach that stage until the kid is about fifteen. Imagine the damage that can be done if parents aren't informed of the stages of development their children are going through. Inappropriate expectations are made at wrong times in their children's lives.

Eric Ericson developed an intricate developmental theory that covers the entire life span. He identified psychological conflicts that must be resolved in order for one to successfully proceed through life's stages. At each stage of life, according to Ericson, you are confronted with psychosocial crises that you must work through. We have all heard about folks that are apparently either in a specific stage of life or in transition from one stage to another. The "midlife crisis" is a perfect example. Toddlers, schoolchildren, teens, young adults and older adults approach life very differently from each other and have different concerns to address. By understanding the theories briefly outlined in the following chart, you can see what you are undergoing in your life and what is yet to come. The chart is in no way complete, but suggests themes that are posed by the theorists discussed above.

The Patterns in Developmental Stages

Stages of Development Related to Age	Sigmund Freud's Psychosexual Development	Jean Piaget's Cognitive Development	Eric Ericson's Psychosocial Development
From birth to about 1 yr. or 18 months old	Oral Stage: Everything goesin the mouth	Infants rely on their physical senses to relate to and understand the world	Understanding of the world comes from interaction with parents and whether the child can trust them to take care of his/her needs
From about 1 year or 18 months to 3 yrs. old	Anal Stage: Fascination with bowel and bladder control	Language skills develop and symbolic thinking develops	Child develops a will and interests of his/her own
From about 3 to around 6 yrs. old	Phallic Stage: Fascination with own genitals	Interest in why things are the way that they are	Initiative and the courage to venture forth develop; desires to undertake and complete tasks alone
From 6 or 7 yrs. old to puberty	Latency Stage: Girls prefer to be with girls, and think boys are icky; boys prefer to be with boys and think girls have cooties	Appropriate use of logic to solve problems that apply to actual objects, but not abstract concepts	Self-awareness and a desire to do things correctly emerge; concern with meeting expectations of others
From 11 or 12 yrs. to around 18 yrs. old	Genital Stage: Heterosexual feelings develop and mature	Develops ability to think abstractly	Self-identity and role in life is explored often with much confusion
From about 18 yrs. to maybe 40 yrs. of age			Desire to fit in is replaced with search for a life-mate to prevent isolation
From around 40 to about 65 yrs. old			Interest in doing something worthwhile in life, contributing to society and guiding the next generation
From about 65 yrs. old onward			Critically review life and feel good about self or despair

We are never through growing and changing from the moment we are born until we leave this earth.

– Don Osborne

Stages of Commitment

Rachel dreamed of the ideal career. An "A" student throughout college, she took her time looking for the right job after graduation. When offered a position with a prestigious firm she was ecstatic. She was convinced that she would spend the rest of her life climbing the corporate ladder within this company and one day be its CEO. She went to work early, often skipped her lunch break and stayed late. After several months, however, it became clear that all of the people above her in the organization were not equally impressed with her performance in a particular area. She felt devastated when one of the upper managers suggested that she take some additional college courses to improve her understanding in an area where she was weak. Rather than put the suggestion in perspective and maybe seek a mentor within the company, she became sullen and began thinking that she wasn't being appreciated for her extra work. She stopped coming in early or working late. Her attitude deteriorated and soon she began taking days off work to look for other jobs. Before long, she found another position with a different company. She resigned her old job and was convinced that her new job was now the perfect opportunity for her. She told her family and friends that she had finally found the company where she expected to spend the rest of her career.

The Patterns in Developmental Stages

Mark Norman, a consultant that I have been privileged to know, describes the stages of commitment to relationships, including to both people and jobs. When you first start a new job, or meet someone new, whether a friend or a romantic interest, there is an initial infatuation period, followed by a routine which may become boring. You then usually enter a period where you notice negative characteristics and become disillusioned and dissatisfied. You may then start looking around and comparing your situation with other possibilities. Ultimately, you must commit to the job or the person, or you will move on, usually to another similar situation and begin the cycle again.

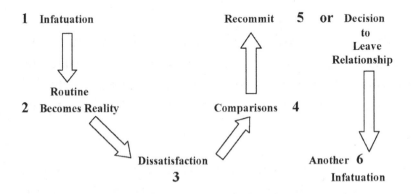

During the **First Stage**, everything is new, hope and expectations are high, and you may think that you have found a perfect situation. If it is a new job, then you might believe that this is the best opportunity you have ever encountered. Like Rachael in the opening story you may think that this will be where you want to spend the rest of your career. If it is a new friendship, then perhaps you see positive traits in your new friend that aren't even there. You may want to spend a great deal of time with your new friend because they seem to be so interesting and accepting of you. Maybe you have some common interests that you exaggerate to think are closer than they really are. If you have entered a new romantic relationship, then you may be blind to any faults that the other person has. You may be truly infatuated and want to spend every possible moment with them. You may foolishly enter a sexual relationship before you know very much about them.

In the **Second Stage**, you have become familiar with your new relationship with the individual or the company you have gone to work for, and settled into a routine. The newness wears off. Your expectations begin to drop in the light of reality. You may grow bored.

As you move into the **Third Stage**, you may grow restless and dissatisfied with the relationship. Faults that you didn't see before now become glaringly these stages and where anyone is in the cycle makes it easy to predict what is likely to happen next. By becoming aware of stages like this, you can alter your choices. You can change the ultimate outcomes in your own life and in the lives and circumstances of the people around you.

Developmental Stages of Groups and Teams

Teams and work groups develop along easily observable and predictable stages. Prior to a group working together, however, there is always some way that the members are selected. Perhaps they voluntarily get together because of a common interest. It may be that some authority in their lives appoints them. Regardless of how people find themselves in a group or on a team, they will still go through the same stages or they will disband. Bruce Tuckman described a developmental model of groups that includes five inevitable stages that are necessary in order for groups to achieve their objectives. Tuckman's stages are sometimes referred to as the "Forming – Storming – Norming – Performing – Adjourning" developmental model.

Forming - In the first stage, members form the group with a greater degree of formality and courtesy than they may display toward each other later. Group members typically seek acceptance from each other, and controversy or conflict is avoided. During this obvious. You might start finding excuses to spen[d] less time at your job or with your friend or lover.

Disillusioned that this is not turning out to be th[e] perfect situation that you thought, in the **Fourth Stag[e]** you may start playing the field, looking for other op[-] portunities. You begin comparing your current circum[-] stances with what you imagine might be possible at [a] different company or with a different person. The mor[e] that you compare your current situation to some othe[r] imagined ideal, the worse you feel.

Ultimately, you are faced with a decision. In the **Fifth Stage**, you must choose to either get out of a situation that has become miserable, or you must commit to seeing this one through. Unfortunately, there seem to be more people choosing to leave jobs and personal relationships and chase other unrealistic fantasies elsewhere. If you confront your dissatisfaction directly, you might see your own contributions to any friction that has developed. If you commit to working things out, you can resolve conflict and your expectations might mature.

You might recognize that your personal happiness comes from within. It is not solely dependent on external factors like the job you hold or the people in your life. Careers, marriages and other relationships might last much longer. The stages described here may be recognized in your own life and/or observed in the lives of other people you know. Recognizing

The Patterns in Developmental Stages

stage, members try to develop rapport with each other, and perhaps show off their area of expertise in order to jockey for their position or role in the group. Most of their focus is somewhat superficial as they decide how often they will meet, how to organize themselves, who will volunteer to take responsibility for what, etc. Because they avoid any conflict, the group members do not address anything that might be controversial or for which anyone may hold strong opinions. If anyone has been appointed or elected to a position of leadership for the group in this stage, then that individual will tend to be directive and talk more than anyone else in the group. The group is not yet able to work together as a team; instead, they are just functioning as a collection of independent individuals.

Storming - Before long every group merges into the next stage. It is called "storming" because opposing opinions are expressed and controversy develops very naturally. Group members may have different ideas about how to approach their objectives and how to define their overall goals. They may disagree on how decisions will ultimately be made, and who gets to work on various parts of the larger project. Some groups experience more unpleasantness than others during this stage, depending on the willingness of the members to work through their differences. Some groups never get beyond this stage and very little gets done or members quit the group. This stage is necessary, however, in order for the group of independent individuals to develop into a collaborative team that actually works together as a unit. An environment of patience and tolerance for opposing views must develop. Recognizing that opposing ideas can result in new, creative solutions is essential. Different views must become welcome instead of resisted in order to progress to the next stage.

Norming - Once group members arrive at a way to accept differences and incorporate them, then the group becomes a team. Some members may give up their own ideas because they recognize that someone else's idea better serves the purpose. Rather than insisting that their own plan be adopted, individuals agree with each other about what is best for the team to function. Everyone takes responsibility for the outcome of the team's efforts. The members have by now formed an open system. They are now in a position to actually make some progress.

Performing - If the group makes it to becoming a true team, then their performance becomes efficient and they develop an interactive style of functioning. They may still offer opposing viewpoints, but they will have established an effective way of incorporating differences into their creative solutions. Functioning as an open human system, the team members feel comfortable expressing themselves and working with each other. Their effectiveness reaches a peak and observers may call them a "high-performing" team at this point. The team itself becomes the decision-making unit, and leadership is shared among the

The Patterns in Developmental Stages

team members. If members leave the team for any reason and are replaced by new members, then the team dynamics will change. They may revert to being a group again and may have to go through the earlier stages all over.

Adjourning - Some teams are formed for a particular project. Once the objectives are accomplished, there may not be any reason for the team to stay together. As the team is adjourned, there will likely be some feelings of loss and separation. After the investment that the members made in order to develop from a group of independent individuals into a unified team, they may feel reluctant to disband. They may express a great deal of pride in what they accomplished together and not want to lose that feeling. If the team must disband, it is very helpful for them to celebrate their success together and be recognized and appreciated for what they did. If their adjournment is planned with appropriate praise from whoever appointed them, then the team members can separate more easily. They then will carry the experience of their success with them and more readily work with future groups on other projects.

Stages of Separation, Loss and Grief

When I first met Jackie, over thirty years ago, she was a young nurse, full of enthusiasm, and a zest for life. She and her husband had just found out that Jackie was pregnant with their second child. The couple was active in their church and quite popular in their circle of friends, which included my wife and me. Jackie was highly regarded for her nursing skills and was quickly promoted at work and given first choice on special projects for the doctors. She always had a smile and patients loved her. She was a petite bundle of energy and very pleased to be pregnant again. It was then that she was diagnosed with multiple sclerosis, an incurable disease that gradually destroys the nervous system. She was in shock at first. I saw her cry a few times but then she became angry. I heard her ask in a private moment, "Why me?" Being a religious person, she prayed that the diagnosis would turn out to be incorrect. Further tests confirmed that she had MS and her pregnancy was at risk. For a little while, Jackie slipped into a state of depression, but then told us "It's okay. I can do this." She meant that she could accept reality, adapt and live with what she could not change. She delivered a healthy baby and over the next twenty years Jackie's nursing career was filled first with exciting opportunities. Then her life began to wind down as the disease took its toll and she no longer had the stamina to make it through a day. She began to limp, dragging one foot behind her and struggled to keep up. Finally, the time came when she no longer had the coordination to drive a car and

The Patterns in Developmental Stages

had to give up her career. Having been fiercely independent all her life, it hit her hard. She struggled over it, got angry, allowed herself to feel the sadness, and then sorted through it. Again, she said, "It's okay. I can do this." And again, she accepted the reality of what she could not change and adapted with an attitude of optimism. She was going to make the most of the life she had left. No longer able to work or even run errands, she was stuck at home. The kids were grown and gone. One day, Jackie's husband of nearly twenty-five years told her that he wanted a divorce... and then he was gone. Jackie was shocked at first, then angry, and then depressed again. She felt sorry for herself for a little while, then, she sorted through it. She told us, "It's okay. I can do this." She moved into an apartment, and lived alone with her cat for the next few years. Her grown children were scattered and didn't live nearby, so friends and relatives took her shopping, and occasionally my wife and I treated her to dinner at a local restaurant. Living alone, she relished time to visit with people that would interrupt the loneliness and boredom of being trapped without companionship, a career, or a car. The once energetic, vivacious woman is now scarcely able to walk, and her hands are too unsteady to write or type on a keyboard. Recently, Jackie told us that she has finally become convinced that she can no longer live independently. She is preparing to move in with others who will help take care of her. She is slowly filling her days packing her few belongings, and she has found a neighbor who will take her cat. At first, the idea of losing her last vestige of independence depressed

Jackie. She allowed herself some time to feel the sadness and the anger, and then she thought it through. My wife and I took Jackie out shopping and to dinner and she talked to us about adapting to her newest loss, and then she smiled the same smile that used to win the hearts of her patients and said, "It's okay. I can do this."

Everyone experiences losses in their lives. Jackie's life is an example of one who has experienced the stages of grief and loss many times. Whenever you lose something that you cherish, whether it is a loved one, a job, your health, your freedom, a significant relationship or a marriage, you will go through five stages first described by Dr. Elizabeth Kübler-Ross in her book *On Death and Dying*. The stages do not always follow one another in sequence, and people can slip from one stage into another and back again. The following are brief descriptions of the stages.

Denial – Usually, the first reaction to a loss is shock and a feeling that "this can't be happening." People often report feeling numb. It is how you are psychologically protected from feeling the whole experience all at once.

Anger – Often, anger is misdirected when a loss occurs. You may be angry with God, or even angry with someone who has died because they left you. It doesn't have to make sense. Sometimes we look for someone to blame and be the target of our anger. Anger frequently covers the underlying pain of the

The Patterns in Developmental Stages

loss. It is easier for most of us to cope with anger than emotional pain.

Bargaining – You may enter a stage where you try to bargain away the loss. If only the manager who fired me will get fired herself, the company will see that I was treated unfairly and hire me back. If only God will wake me up from this terrible nightmare, then I will devote my life to helping others. If only I am given another chance, I will never treat my loved one so badly. If only… You may feel guilty for some contribution to the loss, whether it is real or imagined.

Depression – As the reality of the loss sinks in, you are likely to become depressed. This is not a cause for anti-depressant medication or psychiatric interventions. Depression is a natural reaction to grief and loss and must be felt and worked through.

Lois was in her late 60's when her family took her to a detox center for alcoholism treatment. In truth, she drank very little alcohol, but she did drink daily. The reason she appeared to be so intoxicated each evening was because she was also taking prescribed tranquilizers that multiplied the effects of alcohol. In the process of gathering historical background information on Lois, she reported that she had been on tranquilizers or barbiturates ever since she was seventeen and reacted very emotionally at her father's funeral. For fifty years, she had been medicated from feeling the natural grief at the loss of her father. Once Lois was detoxed from alcohol and sedatives, she began crying over her father's death. The grieving process had merely been suppressed, not eliminated. She began to get well once she was allowed to feel and work through the normal grief reaction. That was a part of her successful treatment for her addiction to sedatives and alcohol.

Acceptance - Although not everyone reaches the final stage, eventually most people arrive at an acceptance of the reality of their loss. You may not like it, but you adapt to the fact that your life has changed and you move on.

When feeling overwhelmed by the blows of Life, permit yourself some time to feel the feelings. Then, remember Jackie and sort through your situation. Talk with friends and loved ones about it until you resolve it, and can adapt to what you cannot change. You, too, can do this!

Stages of Organizational Development

Businesses and other organizations develop through distinct stages in the same way that people develop through the stages of life. Each stage has its own challenges and limitations. Just as parenting teenagers differs from parenting toddlers, organizational leaders and managers must adapt their strategies to meet the needs of their companies as they grow and evolve. Disastrous results frequently occur when organizations do not recognize the stage that they are in and try inappropriate strategies. Each developmental stage requires different leadership and management strategies in order to advance the organization toward the next stage. Just doing "more of the same" is not a successful way to manage a company through planned growth and the resolution of structural problems.

If the senior management and leaders of organizations do not understand the natural evolution of the companies they run and adapt appropriately to meet each stage, then the organizations may fail. Changes in technology, markets, legal and economic environments force companies to adapt in order to survive. If we think of once-prosperous companies like Woolworth's, Sharper Image, Polaroid, Bethlehem Steel, Commodore Computers and Pan American Airlines, we can see examples of large organizations that did not successfully adapt. They are now out of business even though other companies at one time tried to copy their "best practices".

A key concern of businesses is sustainability, and if leader-managers are not well versed in the stages of organizational development and the transition challenges between stages, then their companies can face the same fate. There may be subtle differences from one kind of business or organizational structure to another, but failure to understand the patterns that they undergo creates real problems that could be avoided.

It was my privilege to consult with two very successful businesses that had both reached the limits of their infrastructure. Their sales were outstanding, yet both companies faced disaster if they didn't make some very significant changes in the way that their organizations were structured and run. In talking with the leadership of company "A", they were shocked by my suggestion that they were facing serious trouble and perhaps even going out of business if changes were not made. They intended to just keep doing what they had been doing that resulted in high sales in the belief that their income stream would overcome all problems. A couple of months later, the president/CEO of company "A" sent me a message saying that further investigation on their part confirmed what I had told them and they were instituting the changes that had been recommended. Thereafter, their organization moved into the next stage of development successfully and they continued to grow. Today, they are the country's largest and most successful business in their field.

The Patterns in Developmental Stages

After consulting with company "B", the leadership was incredulous that they could really be in serious trouble because of their high sales. They were somewhat offended by my suggestion that they would go out of business within the next two years if they did not make appropriate changes to their organizational structure. I wished them the best and went on my way. Two years later, they sold off all of their business divisions in order to avoid bankruptcy. They were unwilling to look at the principle of increasing complexity that occurs as organizations evolve over time. The leadership of company "B" was unaware of the necessary adaptations that must be made in organizations to accommodate growth and to adjust to changes in the market and the economy. Today, they are no longer in business.

Various business experts suggest that organizations undergo anywhere between four and seven stages of growth and development. Most of them favor a four or five stage model. For example, Michael Masterson describes four stages of growth he sees as common to every business in his book *Ready, Fire, Aim*. Larry Greiner identifies five stages of organizational evolution (slow steady growth) and revolution (upheaval). Martin and Stupak suggest that organizations develop through four stages with specific benchmarks that define each stage. Each stage has its own problems, challenges, and opportunities. For example, in a start-up situation, there is a greater need to sell the goods and services that the company provides in order to remain in business than there is the need for a well-designed Human Resources department. Another common mistake is to go public and sell stock when the company is not yet structured or ready to do so.

Not-for-profit organizations differ somewhat in their focus from for-profit businesses, but still undergo distinct stages of development. As they mature, both kinds of organizations must struggle with the tendency to burgeon into bureaucracies that lose sight of their original purpose. Departments whose job was to generate and deliver some service or product can become consumed with the need to justify their size and budget. Departments may become "silos" that do not share readily with other departments. That can be seen easily in the US government where a number of departments, bureaus and agencies in the same field have their own budgets. They spend much of their resources making sure that their budgets are not cut, instead of collaborating with other government and private agencies to address the problems for which they were originally created. The following chart incorporates several different models of organizational development for a typical business.

The Patterns in Developmental Stages

Stage	Challenges	Leadership/ Management Approach	Organizational Structure	Requirements to Transition to the Next Stage
Start-Up with $0 to $1million gross revenue primarily from local markets	Make first sale and develop a customer base; establish presence in market	Personal vision of risk-taking entrepreneur; matching business to owner's skills	Business ownership structure determined; initial business planning; "family" style organization	Sell enough to stay in business; stabilize and establish order out of chaos
Small Business with $1 million to anywhere between $3 million and $10 million gross revenue from local and perhaps some regional markets	Growth to increase cash flow and profitability; add products or services	Autocratic, hands-on management with some cross-functional managers assisting	Vertical hierarchy; procedures are established; formal accounting system is necessary; expertise to make sophisticated financial forecasts becomes increasingly desirable	Everyone must buy in to owner's vision; prepare to move from: (1) autocratic to transformational leadership style, (2) from vertical to horizontal management style, (3) from "family" style to scientific management with a strategic plan
Middle Market Business with anywhere between $3 million and $10 million to $50 million gross revenue from some local and more regional markets	Expansion to broader markets; ability to adapt to market changes; capitalize on new opportunities; seek and promote intrapreneuerial opportunities	Team development with experts assuming responsibility for functional domains; owner leads / team manages	Decentralized flattened management structure; depersonalized management style; sophisticated HR department is necessary	All systems must be updated and prepared for organization to run itself with professionals at the helm; plans are developed to face any and all contingencies
Mature Business with $50 million or more in gross revenue from regional, national and perhaps international markets	Sales may slow; organization may become bureaucratic; entrepreneurial spirit must be revived or company begins dying	Interdependent functional teams must run the company; lean management practices; determine owner's new role	Organization must develop its own most efficient systems and forms of operating based on any of several different models	Owner prepares to: (1) reduce own role to Chairman of the Board, or (2) take the company public, or (3) sell it

Stages of Moral Development

The "green energy" company Solyndra was granted over half a billion dollars in federal government loans at interest rates far below what other companies were able to get. A year later most of the money could not be accounted for, they filed for bankruptcy and investigations suggested a scandal that involved government and business leaders alike. When the corporate scandals of the first decade of the 21st century were made public ten years earlier, there was widespread outrage in the USA. Enron and other organizations were charged with fraud, their corporate officers were indicted and once-prosperous corporations were forced into bankruptcy. Thousands of people lost their jobs and pensions. People lost billions of investment dollars, just as taxpayers lost the government's investment in Solyndra. Could any of this been predicted in advance?

Kenneth Lay, the CEO of Enron, was interviewed and quoted many times during the four years that the US government prosecuted him, leading to his conviction and prison sentence. At times, he seemed bewildered by how negatively he was being regarded. He held a PhD in Economics, had been a very successful corporate executive, and had even been considered for appointment as the US Secretary of the Treasury prior to the scandal that led to the collapse of Enron. Kenneth Lay appeared to justify the Enron executives' corruption and fraud with the belief that the ultimate end would

The Patterns in Developmental Stages

have been continually increasing wealth for everyone who invested in or worked for Enron. The end would justify the illegal means. And that may have been the case had he and the other guilty corporate officers not been caught. That then raises enormous ethical questions. Does the end justify the means? Is it still wrong if you aren't caught? How can a highly educated and experienced successful corporate executive hold such a moral code? Isn't that the kind of thinking that drug dealers, bank robbers and other criminals have?

Government officials and corporate executives may receive a great deal more publicity when their moral failings result in thousands of other people being affected. But, it's the same underlying character issue exhibited by many people from all walks of life. Like other areas of your life, your moral development grows through stages that have most notably been researched by Lawrence Kohlberg. Unfortunately, many of us never develop through all of the stages. Kohlberg identified six stages of moral development. The first few stages may parallel other areas of human development, but it appears that many people never grow beyond that. The following is an abbreviated explanation.

Stage One – Kohlberg describes the first stage of moral reasoning as common to young children, although some adults appear to be stuck at this stage. In it, the individual makes decisions based on what consequences they may face if they are caught. Actions are considered "bad" if a punishment follows. The more severe the punishment, the worse the behavior is considered.

Stage Two – In the second stage of moral development, reasoning is based on a self-centered "What's in it for me?" viewpoint. Behavior is considered appropriate according to the benefits the individual will receive as a result. Concern for others is limited to how they may be of benefit to one's own ends. Right and wrong are considered to be relative to the circumstances or situation. "If the action benefits me, then it's good."

Stage Three – Prior to the development of the youth culture, adolescents usually reached the third stage of moral development. In this stage, people behave with a desire to be approved of and accepted by others. Rules of society are followed because it will result in the individual being considered a member of society in good standing. Acceptance is too important to not go along with the majority.

Stage Four – In the fourth stage of moral reasoning, people follow society's rules for the sake of maintaining order and doing what is best for society as a whole. What is in the best interests of a functional society becomes more important than the interests of any one individual. The belief is that law and order must be maintained.

Stage Five – America's fight for independence was based on the moral reasoning of Kohlberg's fifth stage

The Patterns in Developmental Stages

of moral development. Laws are considered appropriate when they meet the needs of the greatest number of people for whom the laws are made, and should be changed if they don't. The Founding Fathers of the United States, for example, rejected laws imposed on them by the English Crown because they were unfair and did not serve the colonies' interests. The revolutionary Americans rejected the laws that only served the interests of Great Britain and established laws for themselves that met the needs of the people that lived in the colonies. Stage five moral reasoning agrees with the need for law and order, but insists that the laws be changeable according to the needs of the people for whom the laws are written. Laws and rules should be determined by the people who must live with them.

Stage Six – Kohlberg found few examples of people that consistently operate at the sixth stage of moral development. In this stage, people live by a code of ethics based on universal truths that go beyond or transcend the laws of men. The reasoning is that there are some things that are wrong and should not be done whether there is a rule or law that says it is okay or not. For example, just because slavery was legal at one time, it was still morally wrong. At the same time, some things should be done because they are the right thing to do, regardless of whether anyone else thinks so. As a result, there is a willingness to break laws that are unjust. This stage of moral reasoning can sometimes be confused with the lower stages of development in which society's rules or laws are ignored out of self-centered personal interests. In stage six moral reasoning, society's rules or laws may be disregarded because it is in the best interest of someone else that needs help. Ideally, rules and laws should maintain social order while also protecting everyone's rights. The civil disobedience of Mohandas Gandhi, Martin Luther King, Jr. and Nelson Mandela are examples of breaking unjust laws in order to advance the rights and standard of living of oppressed and disenfranchised parts of society. Their actions were based on a belief in an absolute set of values of right and wrong. For example, it is always wrong to oppress and exploit other people just because someone has the power to do so. It is always right to stand up and advocate for abused children who are powerless to defend themselves.

Let's revisit the examples of government officials and corporate executives who defraud the public for their own interests. We can see that their moral reasoning reflects the second stage of Kohlberg's moral development model. Relativists do not recognize that there is a right and a wrong regardless of whether they are caught. People who believe in absolute truths believe that some things are always wrong and some things are always right.

"If you succeed in cheating someone, don't think that they are a fool. Realize that the person trusted you much more than you deserved."
– **Anonymous**

The Patterns in Developmental Stages

It makes sense that your personal life and your public or career life are always congruent or in alignment. If you are dishonest in your career or public life, then you are likely to be dishonest in your personal life, too, because all behavior reflects thinking and worldview. If you rationalize immoral behavior in your personal life, then you will also rationalize immoral behavior in your public life or career.

People are capable of changing though. Observing an individual's choices and behavior at a point in time may be different from how they once behaved when younger, or how they might behave later in life.

> You can grow and mature, and you can also regress.
>
> — *Don Osborne*

Key Points & Action You Can Take

You and the groups and organizations that you are in undergo stages of development that are so regular that they are very predictable.

1. The physical stages that we human beings undergo are characterized by changes in your body and physical functioning that are easily observed throughout your entire life span. Understanding the developmental stages that all people experience should prepare you for what the future has in store for you and for your children as they grow and mature. Expectations should be realistic based on what you and your children's bodies are capable of doing during any particular stage. Think about your expectations for yourself and others. Do you need to adjust any expectations to fit reality?
2. Parallel to your physical life stages, you undergo stages of psychological and intellectual development as well. Again, you can fairly accurately predict when you, your loved ones and others you know will experience various changes and challenges. Observe the people around you. Can you see the stage of development that they are in psychologically and intellectually?
3. In addition to the developmental stages you undergo, you will experience other predictable patterns during your life. Perhaps you can see them in others more easily than you can see them in

yourself. You approach changes in relationships with people and career opportunities in predictable ways. If you recognize a pattern of noncommitment in another person, you may choose not to hire that individual or pursue a romantic relationship with him or her. If you do, you can predict what will probably happen. Is there a commitment pattern you need to change?
4. Groups of people undergo observable patterns of development before they become functional teams. Often the process is very challenging. Leaving the group does not solve the problem. Some areas of growth in our lives must simply be undertaken and seen through to their logical conclusion. There isn't always an easy way out. Are you in a group that needs to become a functional team? Share with others what you have discovered about team development.
5. You experience the stages of grief and loss in predictable ways. You may get stuck along the way and not resolve something right away. If you are stuck and unable to resolve a stage that you are in, talk it through with another caring person. It can usually help you move on. Is there someone undergoing the grieving process that you can listen to in order to help them?
6. Whole organizations also develop along predictable stages of growth. If the people responsible for leading and managing an organization are not familiar with what must occur in each stage, the results can be disastrous for the organization.

7. By observing people and the things that they say and do over time you can generally determine their character or level of moral reasoning. You can then predict what they will probably do in given situations. If you discover that someone in a position of power and authority has not developed morally, then you may want to avoid that person or organization, or vote that individual out of office.
8. Examine your own moral development. Which of the six stages do you operate from most frequently? Is the moral stage you operate from consistent with your self-image, the way that you see yourself? Ask others that know you and are willing to be honest with you which stage of moral development they think you operate from most often. Do you want or need to change that?
9. It is important to realize that people change over time. Sometimes you may remain on a particular path or be stuck at a level of development or growth in some area of your life. Some of us undergo changes in our worldview that result in our taking very different paths.

Principle Seven

Whom Do You Serve?

When my wife and I moved to a new location, we called the local satellite TV service to come install one of their units. When the installers arrived, they said that our home was situated so that a clear beam from the satellite was impossible. They could not guarantee that we would receive a signal. We thanked them and chose to have a cable service installed instead. Not long thereafter, we received a bill from the satellite TV company. They charged us for the installation that did not occur, and for the first month's service that we did not receive. We called the company and explained that we did not get their service and to please correct their accounting. We were assured that the problem would be corrected. The next month, we received another bill *and a warning that we were delinquent. Again, we called and explained the truth of the matter to someone in management for the satellite company. Again, we were assured that a correction would be made. The next month, the bill came with a threat of legal action which would affect our credit rating. Now, perhaps some of that fiasco could be blamed on inaccurate data entry in their computer system and then further computer problems, but it felt like no one really cared about the outcome but my wife and me.*

> # Is customer service better or worse than it was in the 1960's and early 1970's?

There is no such thing as an action without any consequence. Generally, "good" actions reap good results, and "bad" actions reap unpleasant consequences sooner or later. However, one of our most common challenges in western organizations is short-sightedness...not looking far enough ahead to see what a course of action will have as an ultimate outcome. Much of what may determine eventual outcomes is the motivation behind any course of action. For whose benefit is the action taken?

Whom Do You Serve?

In the 1980's, organizations like General Electric, led by the highly regarded CEO Jack Welch, decided that the primary purpose of business is to make profits for their stock shareholders. This led to a transition in management philosophy in many corporations that began focusing on cost cutting, out-sourcing to cheaper labor markets and a disregard for other stakeholders in their organizations. Thirty years later, Jack Welch called the practice a dumb idea.

Stakeholders and Sustainability

Stakeholders are people that have a stake in an organization's existence and success. Stakeholders include the stock shareholders, certainly. But they also include the customers, the employees, the vendors, suppliers and other companies that do business with the organizations, and the communities in which the organizations operate. Seeing the primary purpose as making greater profits for stockholders has led to scandals in which other stakeholders have been exploited and harmed.

The Enron scandal was mentioned in the last chapter. In order to make the stock more valuable, unethical accounting practices inflated the stock's value unrealistically. When it all came crashing down, everyone lost...billions of investment dollars, thousands of jobs, people's pensions...all were lost because of this misguided philosophy and the lack of moral character of the Enron executives. The Enron executives tried to justify their actions with an argument based in a relativistic worldview. They believed the end goal of higher stock value for shareholders justified the actions that they took. There was no concept of absolute right or wrong. Everything was relative to the success of increasing the stock's value, even if it was inflated and false. There was no evidence that other stakeholders were ever considered.

The long-term effect of this philosophy has had a profound effect on the economy of the USA. Industries from auto manufacturers to shoe companies to computer and other high-end technology companies have shipped their products or parts of their products to other countries to be made by cheaper labor. American jobs have been eliminated in pursuit of the highest profit for the stock shareholders. The former American employees and parts suppliers were one-time stakeholders in those companies.

There is a common documented practice by many large retailers. Let's say that we begin screen-printing tee shirts with catchy slogans on them, and we land a contract with a giant retailer to distribute them. The next year, the retailer will tell us that they want even more of our tee shirts because they are selling well. The catch, though, is that the big retailer tells us that they will only take them from us if we lower our price to them by ten percent. That erodes our own profits, but

Whom Do You Serve?

we cannot refuse. The next year, the same thing happens. The big retailer now wants us to lower our prices to them another ten percent. The only way that we can do that is to buy cheaper tee shirts on which we screen-print our catchy slogans and provide a lower quality product. You can predict where this is going. By the next year, we have reduced ourselves to a low quality outfit turning out inferior products. Sales have fallen off as a result, and the giant retailer wants another price cut which puts us out of business. When asked about this practice, the retailers might simply say, "We're just trying to keep our prices low for our customers." The fact is that they are maximizing their profits at the expense of a vendor company that they drive out of business.

The people on the board of directors of a large American insurance conglomerate took turns serving as the CEO of the corporation with very large salaries. One CEO chose to outsource the customer service department to a company located in another country as a cost savings. The foreign customer service company took customer calls twenty-four hours a day, seven days a week for less money than the insurance company was paying its own customer service department at its headquarters in the USA. Within a year, however, there were increasing complaints by customers. The foreign customer service company worked hard to address customers' concerns. There was an obvious challenge, though, as their employees spoke English as their second language. What's more, they had learned to speak English from British teachers. The English language as spoken by American insurance customers was quite different and so a communication problem existed. That only further frustrated the already-upset customers who were calling. Because of time zone differences, the foreign customer service company did not have access to the corporate problem-solvers needed to address customers' concerns until the day after a complaint was made. It later was discovered that the CEO of the insurance company owned the foreign customer service company. His decision to outsource the customer service department to "save money for the insurance organization" was also a decision to employ his own foreign company to make more money for himself. In the process, the insurance company's customers were worse served than before, and people started cancelling their policies and switching to other insurance companies out of anger and frustration. The CEO's self-serving decision was another classic example of a highly unethical practice although it was technically legal. At the time, there was no law against it. It was rationalized as cutting costs and saving money for the insurance company in order to boost the value of the company's stock. Because of the loss of customers, however, the insurance company began cutting more American employees. Eventually, that CEO retired with a multi-million dollar bonus and the insurance company declared chapter 11 bankruptcy. Another board member was then selected to be the next CEO with an enormous salary during the re-organization.

Whom Do You Serve?

Free enterprise capitalism served the USA well as long as our culture was based on "doing right by everyone." Labor unions arose to combat the poor working conditions and lack of consideration of employees as stakeholders in the early twentieth century. Corrections were made in industry as a result, and national labor laws were passed to protect workers. For a while in our history, business owners, stockholders, employees, suppliers and customers got along within a reasonable balance and the economy of the USA powered ahead of all others in the world.

Organizations that subscribe to the faulty philosophy of increasing stock values at the expense of all other stakeholders, including the customers, have created enormous problems for the American economy. Additionally, they have promoted a thinking process that is relativistic...nothing is wrong unless you get caught, and you can justify any action that is aimed at increasing stock values, regardless of what it does to others. At the time of this writing, stocks are high in value, but millions of Americans are out of work. There is a growing gap between the very wealthy and everyone else. There appears to be a growing social tension because the system is out of balance.

The American economy has always been based on people and companies selling services or products and making a profit. When all stakeholders are considered in the process, that creates jobs, meets the needs and desires of customers, and stimulates a healthy economy. Ignoring any segment of stakeholders, however, always seems to create resistance and far-reaching problems. Therefore, it is a wrong practice. When some of the stakeholders are ignored, then the organization's ability to sustain itself is compromised. Can the company sustain itself and continue long-term? Can it be profitable over a prolonged time period instead of experiencing wild ups and downs?

> **Sustainability is much more likely when there are a greater number of *stakeholders* invested in an organization's continued success.**
>
> *— Don Osborne*

Absolutes and Doing the Right Thing

There are some things that are wrong and some things that are right all of the time. Relativists will disagree with that statement and say that what is right or wrong is relative to the situation. Many thinkers consider that as part of what is wrong with American society. When you acknowledge absolutes, things that are always true, then you can more accurately predict what will eventually happen for any given pattern of choices and action. If, for example, decisions are made that ignore the needs of people that will be affected by the decision, resistance and problems can be expected as a result. Sometimes, what can appear as a benevolent course of action may ultimately have a very negative consequence. In all of your decisions and choices, you would do well to ask yourself who will be served and who may be harmed by the course of action you are contemplating. You can predict the probable future of a company's success and the outcomes of the various stakeholders if you look at the organization's history and determine whom they serve. Do they serve customers, employees, suppliers and the community they are in, or do they primarily serve themselves?

Dr. Greg Ayers developed a thriving dental practice in Greenville, South Carolina. Greenville is the North American headquarters of a number of foreign corporations. Over the years, many of their employees found Dr. Ayers to perform excellent dental work. One

The Probable Future

afternoon, he received a frantic phone call from an upper level Human Resources manager at one of the large corporations headquartered in the area. One of their executives in Ohio was flying in that evening and had broken a tooth en route. Dr. Ayers told them to pick the executive up at the airport and bring him straight to his office, even though it would be well after hours. When the executive arrived in the company limousine from the airport, Dr. Ayers graciously ushered him in and went right to work. The dental practice had grown to include several other dentists and a sophisticated support system with a number of schedulers, dental assistants, receptionists and office workers. Normally, a scheduled appointment would have been made during office hours, and one of the dentists with full support from the staff would see the patient on the next day. This executive, however, was flying in for a high level meeting the next day and had to fly back home immediately afterward. So, instead, Dr. Ayers worked alone that evening for several hours to fix the executive's tooth. Several times, the dentist made sure of his patient's comfort and carried on a friendly conversation throughout the evening. When he was through, the executive was relieved and very grateful for the emergency dental work that had been performed. What's more, he offered to pay the dentist extra for the inconvenience and outstanding service. Greg Ayers refused. He was happy just to provide the solution. Here was the founder/owner of a large dental practice who knew the reason he was in business was to serve his patients. The executive attended his meeting the next day without discomfort. The corporate *headquarters immediately recommended that all of their employees use Dr. Ayers' practice for their dental needs. The dentist recognized that the emergency service he provided that evening was worth more than all of the advertising he could ever afford. He knew whom he served and his practice thrived even more.*

Key Points & Action You Can Take

You can more accurately predict the path of action someone will take if you know whether they believe in absolutes or if they are relativists. You can probably determine their moral development in the process. An organization is made up of people who together determine its path. The values reflected in organizational practices reveal who they serve.

1. Examine the patterns of action taken by the local, state and federal government. Determine who is ultimately being served and who is being neglected.
2. If you are in a position to do business with any company, you may save yourself a good deal of trouble if you investigate how they have treated other people with whom they have done business in the past.
3. Realizing that some things are always true and not situational permits you to make judgment calls without the trap of thinking that it will be different this time, for you. A common pitfall is the self-centered belief that many of us have that, just because a bad outcome occurred for the last 1,000 people that followed the same path we are taking doesn't mean that it will be a bad outcome for us. It probably will.
4. Ignoring the stake that many different individuals, groups and organizations may have in any undertaking will likely make enemies

of them. By considering all stakeholders in any enterprise, you will have a much greater likelihood of success because all of the various stakeholders will work with you so that they too will share the success.
5. Look for individuals or companies that go beyond providing just the service that they advertise. You can predict the service you will receive.
6. If you provide service to others, become someone that people accurately predict will provide outstanding service. You will thrive.

Principle Eight

Living an Intentional Life Has Risks

There is a popular story about a cynic walking along a beach early one morning, contemplating the futility of life. He spies a child picking up starfish that have washed up on the beach, and tossing them back into the ocean. The cynic asks the child what he is up to. The boy says that he is saving the lives of the starfish by throwing them back into the water. The cynical adult then chides the lad by telling him how futile his efforts are. He says there are too many starfish washed up on too many miles of beach all around the world. The man tells the boy that many of the starfish that he throws into the ocean will only wash back up on the *beach again, and that the child's efforts don't make any real difference. The boy picks up a starfish, spins it twenty feet out into the water, then turns to the cynical man and says, "I just made a difference to that one!"*

There are those among us that take life as it comes. They seem at ease and content to enjoy their careers and their families without the burden of an overwhelming ambition or drive to change anything outside of their own lives. Many of those individuals appear to be pretty happy. Then there are other folk who lead their lives intentionally aimed at making some great difference, people who appear driven by ambition or some curiosity that moves them to pursue great goals. Often, if those individuals achieve great things, they are looked up to as being gifted or very lucky rather than recognizing what they had to go through to reach their goals. The differences between the two kinds of people are significant.

Once, a woman who appeared very happy and at ease with her life was confronted by another woman who remarked, "You sure have it easy." The woman to whom the remark was made responded simply, "You wouldn't think so if you knew what I've had to go through." Living an intentional life in order to achieve some ideal or some vision of a better future comes with a great price. It requires that a vision be embraced; it requires a willingness to risk, often complicating the lives of family members; it requires some serious planning, and it requires perseverance when good sense would suggest dropping the vision and moving on to doing something else in life.

Consider the Following Examples

(Many of these examples were found on a website for a class taught at Emory University.)

- *As a young man, Abraham Lincoln went to war a captain and returned a private. Afterwards, he was a failure as a businessman. As a lawyer in Springfield, he was too impractical and temperamental to be a success. He turned to politics and was defeated in his first try for the legislature, was again defeated in his first attempt to be nominated for congress, defeated in his application to be commissioner of the General Land Office, defeated in the senatorial election of 1854, defeated in his efforts for the vice-presidency in 1856, and defeated in the senatorial election of 1858. At about that time, he wrote in a letter to a friend, "I am now the most miserable man living. If what I feel were equally distributed to the whole human family, there would not be one cheerful face on the earth." He was elected in 1860 and became one of our greatest presidents.*
- *Winston Churchill failed sixth grade. He was defeated in every election for public office until he became Prime Minister of Great Britain at the age of 62. He later wrote, "Never give in, never give in, never, never, never, never - in nothing, great or*

small, large or petty - never give in except to convictions of honor and good sense. Never, Never, Never, Never give up." His brilliant leadership of Britain during World War II when Nazi bombs fell on London is legendary.

- Robert Sternberg received a grade of "C" in his first college introductory psychology class. His teacher commented that there was a famous Sternberg in psychology but it was obvious that he would not be another. Three years later Sternberg graduated with honors from Stanford University with exceptional distinction in psychology, summa cum laude, and Phi Beta Kappa. In 2002, he became President of the American Psychological Association.

- Thomas Edison's teachers said he was too stupid to learn. He was fired from his first two jobs for being "non-productive." As an inventor Edison made 1,000 unsuccessful attempts at inventing the light bulb. When a reporter asked, "How did it feel to fail 1,000 times?" Edison replied, "I didn't fail 1,000 times. The light bulb was an invention with 1,000 steps." Edison went on to patent 1,093 inventions.

- R. H. Macy failed seven times before his store in New York City caught on. Now the Macy's Thanksgiving Day Parade is watched on TV each year...a testament to the store's marketing success.

- Rocket scientist Robert Goddard found his ideas strongly rejected by other scientists on the grounds that "rocket propulsion would not work" in the

Living an Intentional Life Has Risks

rarefied atmosphere of outer space. Goddard went on to pioneer the research that led eventually to the USA landing astronauts on the moon.

- An early football expert said of Vince Lombardi, "He possesses minimal football knowledge and lacks motivation." Now the Super Bowl trophy bears his name as a tribute to his success as a world champion football coach. He led the Green Bay Packers to five NFL championships. Lombardi would later write, "It's not whether you get knocked down; it's whether you get back up."

- John Wooden coached UCLA to ten NCAA national basketball championships in twelve years, winning seven in a row. He once explained that winners make the most errors.

- Michael Jordan did not make his high school varsity basketball team as a sophomore. His biography on the NBA website states, "By acclamation, Michael Jordan is the greatest basketball player of all time." He led the Chicago Bulls to six national championships. Jordan later observed, "I've failed over and over again in my life. That is why I succeed."

- Babe Ruth is famous for his past home run record, but for decades he also held the record for strikeouts. He hit 714 home runs and struck out 1,330 times in his career. He said, "Every strike brings me closer to the next home run."

The Probable Future

- *Tom Landry, Chuck Noll, Bill Walsh, and Jimmy Johnson accounted for coaching 11 of the 19 Super Bowl victories from 1974 to 1993. They also share the distinction of having the worst records of first-season head coaches in NFL history - they didn't win a single game.*

- *Johnny Unitas's first pass in the NFL was intercepted and returned for a touchdown. Joe Montana's first pass was also intercepted. During his first season Troy Aikman threw twice as many interceptions (18) as touchdowns (9), and he didn't win a single game. All three quarterbacks are now in the pro football Hall of Fame.*

- *After Carl Lewis won the gold medal for the long jump in the 1996 Olympics, he was asked to what he attributed his longevity, having competed for almost 20 years. He said, "Remembering that you have both wins and losses along the way. I don't take either one too seriously."*

- *Walt Disney was fired by a newspaper editor because "he lacked imagination and had no good ideas." He went bankrupt several times before he built Disneyland. In fact, the proposed park was initially rejected by the city of Anaheim, California on the grounds that it would only attract riffraff. Now, of course, Disneyland is rivaled only by Disney World in Florida for its success.*

- *Charles Schultz, creator of the* Peanuts *comic strip, had every cartoon he submitted rejected by his high* school yearbook staff. Walt Disney wouldn't hire him either. His Peanuts comic strip has been running in syndication in newspapers since 1950.

- The first time Jerry Seinfeld reportedly walked onstage at a comedy club as a professional comedian, he looked out at the audience, froze, and forgot his routine. He stumbled through about a minute-and a half of material and was jeered offstage. He returned the following night and closed his set to wild applause.

- Hank Aaron went 0 for 5 his first five times at bat. He later set the record for career homeruns, a record that stood for thirty years.

- In 1944, Emmeline Snively, director of the Blue Book Modeling Agency, told modeling hopeful Norma Jean Baker, "You'd better learn secretarial work or else get married." Norma Jean changed her name to Marilyn Monroe and became so internationally famous for her career in Hollywood that she is still imitated today.

- At the age of 21, French acting legend Jeanne Moreau was told by a casting director that she wasn't beautiful enough or photogenic enough to make it in films. After making nearly 100 films, in 1997 she received the European Film Academy Lifetime Achievement Award.

- After Harrison Ford's first performance as a hotel bellhop in the film Dead Heat on a Merry-Go-Round,

The Probable Future

the studio vice-president called him in to his office and reportedly told him, "You ain't got it kid , you ain't got it ... now get out of here." Ford became one of the most successful leading men in motion pictures for the next thirty years.

- *Enrico Caruso's music teacher said he had no voice at all and could not sing. His parents wanted him to become an engineer. Instead, he became one of the greatest opera singers of all time.*

- *Decca Records and Columbia Records turned down a recording contract with* The Beatles, *saying that groups with guitars were on their way out. The Beatles became the most famous and best-selling band in history.*

- *In 1954, Jimmy Denny, manager of the Grand Ole Opry, fired Elvis Presley after one performance. He reportedly told Elvis, "You ain't goin' nowhere, son. You ought to go back to drivin' a truck."*

- *Beethoven handled the violin awkwardly and his teacher called him hopeless as a composer. He wrote five of his greatest symphonies while completely deaf.*

- *Henry Ford failed and went broke five times before he succeeded in creating an enormous fortune as a pioneer automaker.*

- *Vincent Van Gogh sold only one painting during his life to the sister of one of his friends for 400 francs (approximately $50). That didn't stop him*

Living an Intentional Life Has Risks

from completing over 800 paintings. In 1987, one of his paintings sold for $49 million.

- *Auguste Rodin's father reportedly once said, "I have an idiot for a son." Described as the worst pupil in the school, three times he was rejected admission to an art school. Perhaps you've seen images of one of his famous sculptures called* The Thinker.

- *Critics and an angry audience booed Igor Stravinsky after the first performance of the ballet* Rite of Spring *for which he wrote the music. It is now considered one of the great musical masterpieces.*

- *Leo Tolstoy flunked out of college. He was described as both "unable and unwilling to learn." His novels* War and Peace *and* Anna Karenina *are considered international literary classics.*

- *Eighteen publishers turned down Richard Bach's story about a "soaring eagle." Macmillan finally published* Jonathan Livingston Seagull *in 1970. By 1975, it had sold more than 7 million copies in the U.S. alone.*

- *Twenty-one publishers rejected Richard Hooker's humorous war novel, M*A*S*H. In addition to its eventual success as a book, a major motion picture and a TV show were made based on the book.*

- *Twenty-seven publishers rejected Dr. Seuss's first book,* To Think That I Saw It on Mulberry Street. *He eventually had 60 children's books published, which sold over 200 million copies.*

The Probable Future

- *There is a professor at MIT who reportedly offers a course on failure. He does that, he says, because failure is a far more common experience than success. An interviewer once asked him if anybody ever failed the course on failure. He thought a moment and replied, "No, but there were two Incompletes."*

- *Steve Jobs was fired by the company that he started, and then hired back several years later. Apple is one of the greatest American business success stories because of the innovation that Steve Jobs envisioned.*

- *Bill Gates was a Harvard University dropout that sold computer software products that had not even been developed yet. His company Microsoft made him the richest man in the world.*

> "Only those who dare to fail greatly can achieve greatly."
>
> — Robert F. Kennedy

Vision, Risk, Plans and Perseverance

As seen in the lives of the people above, failures can always be expected to accompany risk. You can choose to live intentionally instead of letting life happen to you, but the observable patterns show that it requires:

1. having a passionate vision,
2. a willingness to take risks,
3. making realistic plans to reach intermediate goals, and
4. having the perseverance to see them through.

When looking to predict achievement, it begins with you having a vision for a better future, whether it is for some scientific invention, artistic creation, a cure for disease, or developing a new and better popcorn. You must be passionate about your vision or else you will probably lack the motivation to see it through. If you are able to enlist others and excite them to embrace the same vision, then that is a mark of one of the most effective forms of leadership called *Transformational Leadership*.

Many people may envision something better for themselves or for others but lack the willingness to take the necessary risks involved to make it come true. Sometimes the risks in pursuing a vision may require taking leaps of faith that can affect your family or others. It may require giving up a job that is a sure thing in order to pursue an opportunity that is not a sure thing at all. As a result, some visions are not pursued because it would require jeopardizing a family's financial stability, require a separation from loved ones for an extended period of time, or some other unacceptable condition.

There is a saying that if we fail to plan, then we are planning to fail. Strategic planning is the development of realistic steps to achieve a vision that some may consider unrealistic. In order to realize a vision, there may be several intermediate goals that must be obtained along the way. Each intermediate goal will take time and resources to achieve it.

A little girl named Brook lost a playmate to one of those cancers that only attacks children. Brook was bewildered and did not have the emotional maturity to process the loss and grief. She became distraught and withdrawn. When she was eleven years old, she announced to everyone she knew that she was going to be a cancer doctor for kids when she grew up. Her parents thought that perhaps that was a part of Brook's efforts to cope with her loss. Five years later, she applied and was admitted to her state's special high school for gifted students. Sure enough, Brook graduated from high school with an academic scholarship to a local university where she majored in pre-med and chemistry. She got married her senior year of college. She was the only graduate from her class to be accepted to medical school. Brook completed her medical studies in four years, having a baby during her third year. Then she

Living an Intentional Life Has Risks

served a three-year residency in pediatrics and had her second child in the middle of it. The US Army paid her medical school tuition, so she served four years of active duty as a pediatrician in the Army. While serving, she contracted two debilitating diseases that threatened her permanent health and her career. When she was discharged, she was a board-certified pediatrician with four years of general practice under her belt. A wife and mother of two and a veteran of the Army, she could finally begin her fellowship in pediatric oncology, fulfilling a vision that she embraced 23 years earlier. She did not lose sight of her vision, and worked through numerous intermediate goals and endured some overwhelming setbacks. That kind of commitment to a vision is rare.

The perseverance to achieve the objectives along the way and stay focused long enough, intently enough to realize the vision is also rare. Brook wanted to quit many times along the way and suffered many setbacks on her way to becoming a cancer doctor for kids. The examples of famous people at the beginning of this chapter illustrate the same rare perseverance. Most of us would give up the vision and quit. Statistics prove that. There is something very different about those of us that can conceive of such an internally motivating vision, take the risks, plan so carefully and persist through all of the setbacks and failures along the way.

You may be passionate about a vision at one stage of your life and then as life circumstances change, the vision may lose its relevance. This may be seen in the lives of young adults who marry and begin families. Their earlier passionate vision was appropriate for early adulthood when they were single, but they re-evaluate their priorities once they are responsible for the livelihoods of others. They become less self-centered and less willing to take risks that would jeopardize their families.

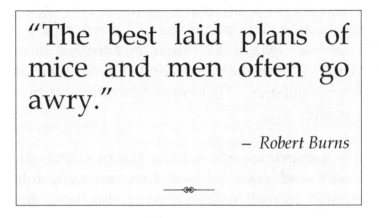

"The best laid plans of mice and men often go awry."

— Robert Burns

Even with all of the passion, planning and persistence, we cannot foresee what Providence has in store. We can use what we know about patterns and proceed with the understanding that not all events are foreseeable.

In the story at the beginning of this chapter about the youngster flinging starfish back into the ocean, the cynical adult may be someone that has suffered a series of setbacks and failures. He may have lost sight

Living an Intentional Life Has Risks

of his own vision, or perhaps has never had a vision of his own. The child has a grand vision of saving starfish. To him, every success, no matter how small, is an encouragement to continue. Not all visions have to be earth shaking. Saving one starfish at a time is do-able. Some will die anyway, but some will live. Success does not have to be saving every starfish on every beach around the world. Success may just be making a difference to one.

Key Points & Action You Can Take

There are significant differences between those among us that take life as it comes and those who lead their lives intentionally aimed at making some great difference. No judgment is due either group. People are wired differently. You can observe the differences in others and recognize them in yourself, as well.

1. Those who choose to let life happen and take it as it comes may just be well-adjusted folk who recognize their own limits and are unwilling to sacrifice their security or that of their loved ones to take high risks.
2. You can choose to live intentionally instead of letting life happen to you, but the observable patterns show that it requires:
   a. having a passionate vision,
   b. a willingness to take risks,
   c. setting realistic intermediate goals, and
   d. having the perseverance to see them through.
3. Failure can always be expected to accompany risk. If you are thin-skinned, have your feelings easily hurt or become overwhelmed with negative feelings when you fail, then pursuing a vision may not be for you.
4. If you have a vision about which you are passionate, and are willing to take the necessary risks to achieve it, you may need help in sorting out the intermediate steps. Often, visionary people are not the best operational planners. If

Living an Intentional Life Has Risks

you're a visionary you may want to seek help in making plans.

5. Visionary people may have to develop positive leadership skills in order to enlist and motivate others to join them in their pursuits. Seek out instruction on leadership development and don't confuse leadership with management.
6. If you know people with strong visions that work alone toward their goals, for example engineers that spend a great deal of time on computers, they may not develop people skills. Taking the Dale Carnegie Course offered by local Dale Carnegie Training companies may be one of the best steps a visionary can take. Warren Buffet did.
7. If a visionary is successful, others may want to take the credit or share in any opportunities for wealth or fame that result. The visionary person may be exploited or robbed of their success. If you or someone you know is a visionary, you may want to take steps to protect eventual success.
8. Discouragement and depression often accompany the many failures that risk-takers experience along the way. Expect it and plan strategies to counter it.
9. A person's worldview is tied directly to their chances of having the personal convictions and a strong enough ego to pursue a vision that may result in failures. Prepare positive input and

The Probable Future

associate with encouraging people to counter the negative messages that failures may give you.

10. If you ultimately experience great success, your worldview may very well change, and you may see yourself quite differently than you did before the success.
11. Consider these patterns that are associated with visionaries when you think about hiring, befriending or marrying one. If you are a visionary yourself, think about the patterns described here and determine if your vision is important enough to you to endure the inevitable hardships and put your loved ones through those hardships with you. Different stages of life may result in a change in worldview and values so that once-held visions lose their importance in the light of life's changes.
12. Even with all of the passion, planning and persistence, even with the wisdom to predict probable outcomes, you cannot foresee what Providence has in store. You can use what you know about patterns and proceed with the understanding that not all events are foreseeable.
13. If you are committed to your vision, no matter its size, remember the words of Winston Churchill, "Never, Never, Never, Never give up!"

Epilogue

Develop the Wisdom to Predict and Change Your Future

Driving through the Southeastern United States, you can see a vine called kudzu growing over other trees and shrubs, outbuildings, parked cars up on cinder blocks, and anything else stationary. It is a weed that covers everything near it, and grows so quickly that it kills the shrubs and trees it smothers. Kudzu is not native to North America. It was introduced at the Japanese pavilion in our country's 1876 Centennial Exposition. Throughout the South, it is now spreading at the rate of 150,000 acres a year. Was the introduction of kudzu to the USA thought through? Could today's infestation been predicted if someone thought about it in the late nineteenth century?

The Probable Future

When thinking of Australia, what do you envision? Kangaroos? Koala Bears? You probably don't think of rabbits. Rabbits are not native to Australia. They were introduced from Europe in the nineteenth century initially for food and kept in pens or fenced in areas. The story goes that someone decided to release a dozen rabbits into the wild for sport hunting. What harm could that do? The rabbits multiplied like...well, like rabbits. Australia did not have the same natural rabbit-eating predators that Europe had. Estimates today are that the last hundred years of efforts to control the pests has reduced the rabbit population from an estimated high of 600 million to about half that many in the early 21st century. Hundreds of millions of rabbits have eaten so much of the ground level vegetation in Australia that they have starved other animal species to near extinction, and created an enormous soil erosion problem. An estimated $600 million is lost annually as a result. Could the devastation caused by releasing a few rabbits into the wild have been predicted?

It's easy to see what should have been done in hindsight. Considering the lessons in the eight principles contained in this book, could you have thought through the potential outcomes of the two scenarios above? Perhaps it would have required some investigative research and some thinking, but that is how probable outcomes are predicted. It begins with seeing patterns in what has happened before.

History is not often a favorite subject of study. By reading history, however, we find much larger patterns over longer periods of time. For example, there have been a number of comparisons written about the Roman Empire, the British Empire, and recognizable similarities in the United States' world influence in the second half of the twentieth and early twenty-first centuries. The earlier empires fell as a result of:

- internal social and moral decay,
- the incompetence of a self-serving ruling elite,
- a wide gap between the wealth of the upper 1% of the population and everyone else,
- a rejection of the fundamental principles upon which the empires were founded,
- the broader culture dividing up into separate ethnic identities instead of assimilating, and
- an acceptance of a broad variety of contradictory viewpoints that became considered equally valid and true.

As a result, the populations of the empires became conflicted, polarized and could not agree on what was in the best interests of their nations. They fell from within. Some see nearly identical patterns in what is happening in the United States, and the future appears to be very predictable. With an awareness of the patterns, however, the probable future can be changed by people who take action.

If a dozen people standing on a street corner observe an auto accident, the police will take statements from each witness individually and independently from the

The Probable Future

others. The reason is that each person will naturally interpret the events that they witnessed through the lens of their own worldview. One witness may say that the car driven by the woman was being driven carelessly, and another may say that the same woman driver swerved to avoid hitting a pedestrian. Others might tell entirely different stories. The police look for the threads of similarity among the different statements in order to find something that just about everyone seems to agree on. That then becomes the consensus reality, or the reality as most of the people saw it. That may or may not be what really happened but most of us check our own perceptions normally against what the majority of the people like us seem to think.

It is certainly possible that most people saw it inaccurately but we must start with an open willingness to question our own perceptions. That is why you must be careful about making decisions when you are upset, infatuated, grieving, angry, excited, or otherwise emotionally charged. Your emotions can override your reasoning with terrible results. You wind up making a decision based on emotion and then using your reasoning to justify it.

> Make no big decisions when emotionally charged.
>
> – *Don Osborne*

Develop the Wisdom to Predict and Change Your Future

As you look at yourself introspectively, you must begin by recognizing that your closely held view of yourself, of who you are, is limited by your inability to see yourself as others see you. Interacting with other people helps you gauge how you come across and tests your perceptions of reality.

In addition to becoming increasingly aware of your own emotions and thinking patterns, you are responsible for what you let into your mind. Since you become what you think about, and since your thinking reinforces your worldview, you can change your thoughts and the outcomes of your life by reprogramming yourself. Spending time with the sort of people that you admire, listening to music or information that is uplifting and positive, watching TV shows or movies that have positive messages, reading about people that are like the people you want to become can all help you reshape your self-image deep in your worldview.

In order to change the probable future, you must examine your past to find the patterns of how you see yourself and how you treat others, and change those patterns as necessary. *You cannot change other people, only yourself.* Then you can change how you respond to various situations you encounter in life.

As you continue seeing the patterns in your own life and then look for the patterns in the lives of other people, families, groups and organizations, they become easier to see. The ability to recognize patterns becomes the foundation of wisdom. You can then begin predicting what will likely happen next with a greater degree of accuracy. Your perspective changes as you ask what will happen next, and then what will happen after that. The development of wisdom is more evident when you use that ability to predict the probable future and make more successful choices than you have in your past. By doing so, you can alter what would otherwise have become your probable future and the future of the other lives you touch.

> You can change the probable future for yourself and the lives you affect by recognizing and changing the patterns in your thinking, your choices and your behavior. Then change how you treat the people around you.
>
> – *Don Osborne*

"So", Krisann asked me as I stopped typing, "Did you recognize any new patterns as you were writing?" "Yeah," I said. "I have trouble writing in normal language. I'm used to writing scholarly papers and not for regular people." "Yes," she said, "but aside from the difference in writing for the academic community and writing for normal folks, did you realize anything else?" "Yes," I replied. "Some people told me that the concepts in the book **The Probable Future** were too abstract for normal folks to grasp. They kept telling me that I had to 'dumb the book down'. They were wrong. A lot of folks read the manuscript and understood it just fine. I had to work hard at putting the concepts into everyday language, and I don't think that I succeeded very well in a lot of places. But the people that will read this book are not dummies. In fact, I think that this book's audience is pretty smart. It's really for everyone, and the people in our country aren't stupid. Maybe they haven't been given some of these ideas to think about before. But many will use them to better their own lives and the lives of the people close to them." "Then, my love," Krisann said, "You have identified the most valuable pattern of all. People will do the right thing when given the right things to think about."

– Don Osborne

References

Bogsnes, B. (2009). *Implementing Beyond Budgeting: Unlock the Performance Potential.* Hoboken, NJ: John Wiley & Sons.

Bronfenbrenner, U. (1979). *The Ecology of Human Development.* Cambridge, MA: Harvard University Press

Carnegie, D. (1959). *Dale Carnegie's Scrapbook.* New York: Dale Carnegie & Associates.

Deal, T. & Kennedy, A. (1982). *Corporate Cultures: The Rites and Rituals of Corporate Life.* Reading, MA: Addison-Wesley Publishing

Erickson, E. & Erickson, J. (1983). *The Life Cycle Completed.* New York: W. W. Norton & Co.

Freud, S. (1905). *Three Essays on the Theory of Sexuality.*

Glasser, W. (1965). *Reality Therapy: A New Approach to Psychiatry.* New York: Harper & Row

Greiner, L. E. (1972). Evolution and revolution as organizations grow. *Harvard Business Review.* Vol. 50(4).

Kohlberg, L. (1973). The claim to moral adequacy of a highest stage of moral development. *The Journal of Philosophy,* 70(18), 630-646.

Kübler-Ross, E. (1969). *On Death and Dying.* New York: Scribner.

Maltz, M. (1960). *Psycho-cybernetics.* Psycho-Cybernetics Foundation.

Martin, S. E., & Stupak, R. J. (2005). Organizational passages: context, confluence, and complexities.

Virtual Strategist, 1 (8) Retrieved January 28, 2007, from http://www.virtualstrategist.net/Issue 8

Masterson, M. (2008). *Ready, Fire, Aim.* John Wiley & Sons.

McGregor, D. (1960). *The Human Side of Enterprise.* New York: McGraw-Hill.

Nightingale, E. (1957). *The Strangest Secret.* (Audio Recording)

Piaget, J. (1952). *The Origins of Intelligence in Children.* New York: International University Press.

Schein, E. H. (2004). *Organizational Culture and Leadership (3rd Ed., Rev.).* San Francisco: Jossey-Bass.

Tiebout, H. (1999). *Harry Tiebout: The Collected Papers.*

Tuckman, B. (1965). Developmental sequence in small groups. *Psychological Bulletin* 63 (6) 384-399.

Schroeder, A. (2008). *The Snowball: Warren Buffet and the Business of Life.* Bantam.

About the Author

As a young man, Don Osborne developed a passionate interest in why people behave as they do, and how some folks are so effective at helping others change and realize their potential. He earned a Masters degree in Counseling (Psychology) and changed careers. During the next several years, he saw over 1,000 individuals and families as clients. It soon became clear that many counseling agencies faced organizational problems as great as the personal problems the clients had. Don founded and served as CEO of a private psychiatric hospital, and later started his own outpatient counseling and consulting agency. As counselor and consultant to a sheriff's department and criminal corrections agencies, he went to FBI training to become a Crisis Negotiator. On one occasion he was called on to talk a gunman into surrendering in front of an elementary school. Don provided group therapy services to incarcerated felons for nine years, decreasing their recidivism rate by over 20%.

In a parallel career in higher education, Don served as an Assistant Professor, Department Head, Area Chair, Associate Dean, and Director of Education for four different colleges and universities. In higher education, as in counseling, his observation was that the institutions were often in as great a need of direction as the students.

Eventually, many of his clients became organizations and the executives that run them. He went

Develop the Wisdom to Predict and Change Your Future

back to school and earned another Master's degree in Advanced Leadership Studies and a Doctor of Education degree (EdD) in Organizational Leadership. His consulting work has included private and public corporations, government institutions and not-for-profit organizations.

Dr. Don Osborne's life work has been focused on helping others identify their greatest challenges and develop strategies to overcome them. People and organizations ususally discover their own potential in the process. Don then motivates and supports them to fulfill that potential. This mission is one that developed over 35 years as a counselor, educator, business owner, manager, CEO, researcher, trainer, and consultant. His research has been on rapid growth organizations, and the effects of *Transformational Leadership* and *Transactional Leadership* training. His current professional focus is on providing leadership development training and coaching, organizational consulting, speaking, and writing. *The Probable Future* is the first book in his **Think Then Lead** series of books which will eventually also include *Manage Less - Lead More,* and *Worst Practices.* Don and his wife currently live in South Carolina. His website can be found at **www.thinkthenlead.com** and he can be reached at **don@thinkthenlead.com**.

Made in United States
Orlando, FL
15 February 2024